WOMEN
of a
CERTAIN
AGE

WOMEN of a CERTAIN AGE

Edited by

Jodie Moffat, Maria Scoda & Susan Laura Sullivan

 FREMANTLE PRESS

Contents

Introduction – Jodie Moffat
with Maria Scoda and Susan Laura Sullivan

I was at a conference recently, at a networking group discussing elder rights, and one of the participants – a woman – said that for the purposes of government policy, to be considered an elder, a person need be sixty-five or older, fifty if you are Indigenous.

I was genuinely surprised. In my mind, an elder was someone wizened and ancient, but apparently, in fourteen years time, I would become that entity: elder. My youngest son celebrated his fifteenth birthday the day before that network meeting. Here I was, balanced on some sort of ridge-cap between mother and crone.

There is no handbook for ageing. Time is unidirectional, impartial, indifferent and unsparing; not all of us will have children, or partners or careers. But we will all age.

I remember being heavily pregnant, half my body weight again, waiting for a woman on the train to notice me and take her son on her lap to give me a seat. These days when I get on the train someone always stands for me; that's what the stick figures on the posters tell us to do: stand for the pregnant, the infirm and the elderly.

I was half the age I am today the last time I was asked for ID at a pub and I thanked the lad on the door for his query. It was always my greeting at pub doors, but these days I get the feeling I have erred by expecting to be allowed entry to a pub at all.

You never feel age, it happens without your permission all the time: one minute being pulled over by a cop because you don't look old enough to drive and the next being unable to read road maps without your glasses.

But even my glasses don't show me how the world sees me at this age; that is something I see reflected in the eyes of others, and in how they treat me. I was always older than I looked, but at some point the big reveal of my actual age stopped being the point at which I gained respect and started being the point at which I became invisible.

I was thirty-odd the first time I was advised with no encouragement or preamble by a salesgirl about products suitable for ageing skin. I was fortyish the first time a doctor told me I should accustomise myself to everyday back pain because it was inevitable, a necessary consequence of having borne two large babies, and age. About that time, hairdressers started asking me what I wanted to do about the grey in my hair: 'Nothing' was implicitly the wrong answer.

Being possessed of a naïve and unshakeable belief in justice, and a blissful ignorance of whether or not the profession would welcome me, at forty I decided to study law. At forty-five I became a solicitor with a respected law firm. After continual positive performance reviews, I thought I had reached a place where I was being judged by my employer solely on my skill set and work ethic. I was nearing fifty; I stopped dyeing my hair and wearing the lipsticks and tight skirts that were no longer flattering, and the high heels that were painful and at times life-threatening. I sought a pay rise commensurate with my experience and revenue-generating capacity.

And that is when it happened. I began to fade. I faded so much that I became a grey smudge in the peripheral vision of my employer, both overlooked and looked through. The younger, brighter solicitors began outstripping me, not in performance but in recognition. I had witnessed older female support staff vanishing from my workplace, one by one, but they weren't money-making legal practitioners as I was. It didn't matter. There was no pay rise. When I left the firm abruptly, with a quick sideways push from the middle-aged male principals, the space contracted around my absence seamlessly, as if I had never been there at all.

I started noticing it elsewhere in my life, a gradual diminution of my presence in the world. In places I had been formerly welcomed, cafes and pubs for example, I became a piece of unwieldy furniture impeding the real customers. My children tripped over me on the way to their lives.

But I was not alone in my pall of invisibility. It became a primary topic in conversations I had with similarly aged female friends. At the crux of one such conversation, my friend Maria suggested we write a book about what was happening to us. I contacted Sue, another friend of our age, and we set up a teleconference to discuss what we could do. In that conversation, this book was born.

Maria, Sue and I agreed we would reach out to a cross-section of women past the age of forty and gauge their willingness to write about things they may or may not have done to arrest the assumptions and presumptions that age deposits on us, like so much dust. Our mandate was simple: we weren't looking for stories about ageing gracefully; we wanted stories that recognised the woman inside and outed her, stories that embraced her.

We were heartened by the positive response and like-mindedness amongst the women we approached. We found that most of the women we spoke with were in the same place as us, a place we had arrived without fanfare and, somehow, unexpectedly. We found that, despite a span of some thirty years in age between our youngest and our oldest contributors, each had grown to have a strong sense of self: some coming to terms with regret, some seeing this time in their life as an opportunity for growth or giving back, some feeling a sense of accomplishment, some feeling a restlessness about what is to come. Many were generous with their time and with advice on how to nurture this idea of a book into a reality. We brought our idea to Fremantle Press where we were welcomed with an extraordinary amount of support and encouragement to bring this book to fruition.

We selected fifteen stories that for us captured the essence of women of our own age and beyond; stories of public achievement, personal development and private reflection. Our book begins with the tale of a woman who did not expect to live to menstruate, let alone reach motherhood and thereafter, menopause. We move through the phases of a woman's life, through androgynous childhood to fertile motherhood and, for some who did not become mothers (and some who did), rich and productive working lives. We hear from women whose lives have been affected by their cultural backgrounds, regardless of any personal preference, and from women who have reached a place where they are older but perhaps not wiser, still yearning to live and become content with themselves. We hear from women who continue to make a difference in the face of indifference. We move through a multitude of experiences to end with an observation of the inevitable ordinariness of life, reconciling oneself to a certain sadness and not recoiling from it.

Each of these stories is singular it its detail, though certain themes, beyond ageing, create links and connections between the different pieces. We hear from women whose challenging childhood has wrought in them a profound capacity for peace and the ability to endure, as seen in the very different narratives of Charlotte Roseby, Goldie Goldbloom and Tracey Arnich.

The idea of a 'typical' Anglo-Australian lifestyle is challenged in migrant stories from Anne Aly, Mehreen Faruqi and Maria Scoda, and examined in two quite different ways in the Indigenous woman's experiences of Jeanine Leane and Pat Mamanyjun Torres. The idealised Anglo-Australian existence is viewed through the prism of lived experience by Jenny Smithson, Pam Menzies and Susan Laura Sullivan, with the latter two providing something of a historical context.

Many of our writers address the quintessential discrimination that exists between men and women, most keenly experienced in the traditional male-dominated workplaces in which Mehreen Faruqi, Jenny Smithson and Anne Aly have prevailed to a greater or lesser degree.

And within this mix are the ordinary, inescapable experiences of women of a certain age. Our bodies betraying us, changing without our consent in ways with which we may disagree; our relations with people around us delineated by how we are seen and not seen. These are the experiences explored in intimate detail by Krissy Kneen and Sarah Drummond, Brigid Lowry and Liz Byrski.

These stories speak to the everyday and sometimes very raw experiences of women of a certain age. We look at the diversity of our lives and are heartened by our commonality and our capacity to endure. Rather than being diminished, we are strengthened by the absence of expectation facing us, and the extraordinary opportunity and unshaped potential this gives us to be exactly whomever we choose.

Just as one conversation between Sue, Maria and I yielded this abundance of personal wisdom and lived experience, it is our hope that these stories will begin conversations amongst readers about what it means to be a woman of a certain age.

Still here still – Charlotte Roseby

I dreamed of funerals like other little girls dreamed of weddings. It would be a big production and, because this was the 1980s, set to my cassette of *Hooked on Classics*, all of us in the processional stepping out to that cracking electronic back beat. This was my party so I got to be alive as well as in the box.

I knew I was about to die. I wasn't sure when, but looking around at the other kids with cystic fibrosis in hospital, the ones looking like skeletons with oxygen tubes stuck in their noses, it looked to me like it was going to be about thirteen. I was twelve.

Most of our medical information was transferred from bed to bed.

Six-bed rooms: teenage girls in one, boys next door; intravenous antibiotics for four weeks at a time.

That we were teenagers was pretty new. Before 1960, a baby born with cystic fibrosis (CF) typically lived just a few months. It had been this way for centuries; in the 1600s these infants were believed to be hexed: 'Woe to that child which when kissed on the forehead tastes salty. He is bewitched and soon must die.'

In the 1970s, eight years was the average survival age. By 1998 it was 29.5. So there we were, right in the middle, rewriting a little corner of medical history.

13

The nurses had cultivated school-camp cool, against boys putting Fanta in their nebulisers to see what happened when you breathed it in, and spitting 'frogs' into cups and tossing them out the windows. Messages and cassettes left under pillows: 'Do you like him?', 'She likes you', 'He wants to pash you', and the Great Raid of September 1985 in which the letters 'R' and 'O' disappeared in the night from the Royal Children's Hospital street sign and we were all threatened with expulsion. Pretty funny given all we wanted was to go home.

A photo shows us dancing on the olive linoleum. Like wartime platoons we formed strong bonds based on survival, friendships as strong and as long as 'lifelong' could be. Baiting each other: bet you can't pierce your own ear with that syringe / sneak out to the cinema / get those antibiotics into your vein in under a minute. Compared to the banality of life outside, these kids were the liveliest, alive-est, kids I knew.

There was a lot to be frightened about. The total sum of effort towards comfort was a poster of Garfield someone had tacked on the ceiling, so you could watch him mouth 'Why me?' right above your head, while they dug around in your arm for a tired old vein they could stick. If you cried you'd be heard through the glass and get mocked by your buddies, and half-mocked by the nurses who'd seen worse, so I'd have to really concentrate on not.

We sometimes debated who was next. As in, who was next. But quietly, because saying things like that would get you into trouble with the nurses.

To think of these kids' lives as being 'terminal' is to miss what went on here, and what they brought to life. Their lives were rich and hilarious and sad and painful and joyous and in all ways, focused. They had been given the gifts of mortality: lack of pretence, intense focus, intense relationships. Enjoying the small moments and making sure they're funny. Attentiveness to life. And the corollary: a falling away of things that aren't important.

They passed those gifts to me and taught me that on the bedrock of the fear of death, a very full life can be built. Staring death in the face wasn't so bad. Just remember to look away most of the time.

We had so much fun that we started to resent hospital visitors.

Each day my mother brought food in a basket. Dad visited in the evenings, so uncomfortable I kept trying to let him off the hook. 'You don't have to come,' I pleaded. He was a pharmacist specialising in mental health. He was dedicated to his patients, but here he was rendered unbendable. He couldn't seem to sit down on a chair or on the hospital bed, so we wandered the empty night-time corridors, getting ourselves lost and riding the lifts up and down in the deserted shopping-mall wards.

'You have to watch it,' he warned me every visit. 'You'll become institutionalised. You'll start loving the place.' He always spoke like this, over the tops of children's heads.

I sort of understood. You offered up your lungs for repair and offered up every little decision at the same time, starting from the moment the nurses woke you, wheeling along a hot breakfast trolley offering baked beans and cold toast. The cleaners arrived each day midmorning to swirl the mop in the toilet and wetly sop the floor. You settled into place so that your bed number was yours and you couldn't imagine it being anyone else's.

My father shouldn't have worried; these hospital corridors gave me a real education.

Joanne started out well enough in the bed next to me. She was a tiny girl with a sharp wit and unmerciful giggling, coughing, giggling. Her bed was the meeting point for everyone else, and she was the centrifugal force. In the middle of the night she started breathing out with noisy sighs. The ins seemed to be okay, if not a little faltering. It was the outs. Grinding. An electric knife in the night. Like giving voice to years of pain in every breath.

I lay there rigid, hoping the night nurses down the corridor would hear what I was hearing. Then I half-woke as they quietly moved her into the isolation room. By the morning, we all knew what that meant. That's where the sick kids went. Or someone studying for their year twelve exams. Either way, serious.

Her big brother sat on the end of her bed and cried while the rest of her family faced front, looking overly interested in the music videos. I'd never seen a teenage boy cry before. So fascinating. My memory of him is firmly embedded along with Bonnie Tyler and Foreigner.

Joanne taught me how you die from a respiratory illness. How I would die. The fast breathing seemed to just rip the weight off. Faster at the end. Joanne sat on her island bed, skinny crossed legs in front, spine curved in a ball. Somewhere under that rounded back there would be nasal oxygen cannulas pressing in the air. I could start to pick the sick ones because they started leaning over.

I realised what Joanne's sounds were, years later. Those ones that pierced the half-darkness of the hospital room.

Cheyne-Stokes breaths (or as I thought at first, 'chain-stoking' – dragging a heavy chain around made perfect sense). Dying people often experience them, to the distress of those around them but of no distress to the one doing the breathing.

Joanne's mother Margaret was just above her daughter's height. A stocky, devout Catholic with lots of children at home and never without her button earrings and a hairbrush. She was a constant presence, stepping out of that isolation room to check in on us all. How are you? How are you doing? I was doing embarrassingly well.

Four days later, Margaret wanted us to be allowed to view her daughter's body, which she had lovingly laid out herself.

It was an extraordinarily generous gesture. The CFs, the anorexics, the depressives, the asthmatics, the diabetics were ushered in; that's how they called us and we called ourselves, two by two.

It was my first real sight of a laid-out dead body, one looking exactly like an angel in a lace and satin full-length nightdress with a pie-crust collar and perfectly straight, brown combed hair and her hands set. I didn't mean to view the body. I just followed Christine in the room because she was fifteen, and I was not quite. Christine probably thought she was saying it inside her head, but she burst into tears and yelled it out loud – 'Yuk!' Joanne's mother was very understanding about that.

Usually, you only knew someone had died because they worked so hard to hide it. A nurse came along and ushered you into whatever room was closest. We all just looked at each other. A lock-in. This was interesting. I'd never even noticed there were doors. They did the long wheel down the corridor with the body, making sure no-one saw. Or, more correctly, making sure no-one would comment. Then a designated nurse took us downstairs to the park for consolation, on the dry, dusty plain of yellow grass. After someone died, a nurse, Peter, gave me a small red leather coin purse that unfurled like a flower. Here you are.

Kelly was hunched over her feet in her isolation room. The position. Rounded back, crossed legs, sucking up that oxygen. She cried, aloud, for days on end. She sometimes howled. I guess while she still could. Behind the safety of the nurses' station, they rolled their eyes to each other and muttered, indignant somehow, 'Oh my god, there she goes again.'

How unprepared, how ill-prepared, those nurses were. How unable to provide anything beyond what was prescribed.

This was the mid- to late-80s, a period of looming medical leaps. The mapping of genes. Isolating the CF gene. The first Australian lung transplant in Melbourne in the early 1990s.

CF was beginning to symbolise all the technologically driven developments of the twentieth century generally. Starbursts of brilliance in a lab somewhere, slowly making their way to the ordinariness of a hospital ward.

There were other changes. Clever antibiotics used much more cleverly. A realisation that kids spending time together in hospital, and sending kids away on jolly CF camps, actually meant they were sharing a whole lot of nasty pathogens – that a separation of bacterial powers was needed to slow down cross-infection rates.

I was starting to survive. I seemed to just gently bump my head against the life expectancy average, and as I grew, so did it. Just lucky at birth I guess.

When we were fifteen, Rebecca and I made a pact to make it to twenty-one. It didn't seem that far away, but the years for her were all just wrong, in the way that they were going right for me.

Rebecca needed and wanted a new-on-the-scene transplant. Her family threw her a jubilant 'six stone party' when she finally managed to put on enough weight for the doctors to begin to consider her for the transplant list. That's thirty-eight kilos.

Six men raised Rebecca up in her coffin. In the flicker of an eye, or maybe just of my eye, it looked like they overestimated the weight and had to lower her back down to their shoulders.

I loved a funeral, enjoyed the ecstatic grandness of the church, the cool and the dark, but not the tinyness of that coffin. I thought about crying, but with my mother next to me, that would be too embarrassing for both of us.

Despite the technological leaps, there was still no way of knowing who would be on what side of the line. You still couldn't pick it for sure. This isn't a 'how long have I got doc?' disease. The trajectory has never been that fixed, which is why a good doctor will appear distantly vague if asked.

There's no success or failure, no winning or losing, no battle. It was a day-by-day constant, unlucky–lucky thing. For this group of kids, it just was. Until it wasn't.

Until what? Until progressive lung infection with more and more acute exacerbations mean that death eventually crowds out life. Infection. Phlegm, mucus, fluid. It's not a cliché to say dying from CF is like drowning. It is drowning.

There is serious work involved in living even a single day with CF. The daily upkeep to keep the lungs clear and the body with enough energy to fight infection: hours and hours of physiotherapy and airway clearance, exercise, nebulisers, puffers, enzymes, antibiotics, mucolytics, high-energy diet, and the burden grows greater the sicker you get. Sometimes five hours treatment for three hours reprieve. Just to set you up for the next day. The tide goes out, it washes in again.

Life and death is imprinted on daily life. This is what makes CF so interesting. You really have to want to live to do all that. If you are talking to someone with CF, you know that they want to be there talking with you. They have worked bloody hard to be there.

'It just must become like brushing your teeth,' people say. No, it never does. The daily regime is a life-affirming, life-wanting act that teeth brushing can only aspire to.

Someone with CF could give it all up, just relax and let it slide, but I've never even heard of that happening. Five hours work a day for a little more living? Ten hours? Sure. Life gets addictive.

CF can give you the rock-star, 'die young, look good in your coffin' blasé attitude for a while, but if you make it past that, what it eventually makes you is extra careful. With all that time and effort invested, risk-taking just starts to look ridiculous. It would be such a waste of all that time and effort to then go and get hit by the proverbial bus (which could still happen, so I'm very careful crossing roads).

I kept surviving. For a while there in my thirties, I

enjoyed pointing out the obvious: 'Well, it looks like I'm going to live.' My cousin Jason was furious because he thought he'd missed some family pronouncement about my ever-impending death – yet again – and stamped his feet: 'No-one tells me anything.' I agreed utterly. No-one told me either. If I'd known I was going to live, what would I have done differently? I can torture myself for hours with that one.

Although I was medically treated the same, it turns out that I was probably just not as sick as those sick kids in the first place. They didn't know then that different genetic mutations for CF give people a range of different outcomes, that for some, CF can be just annoying. I was somewhere in between, stumbling about 'in the kingdom of the well and in the kingdom of the sick'.[1]

Turning forty coincided with a medical pronouncement that I could expect to live for years yet. At twenty-two I'd already felt the sting of old age, and I couldn't put my finger on the strange, anticlimactic portent I felt at this news. 'I know,' said my friend Monique, triumphantly. 'It's disappointment. You're disappointed you're not dying anymore ... Now you have to share death with the rest of us.'

She was right. I'd always thought I would be good at dying. I knew what it looked like. What it would look like on me. Now I'm too late to do it young and I'm too old to do it looking like a beautiful angel.

Yes, now I'm old. Really old – over forty. In CF dog years that's about 106. And I'm as surprised as anyone – as any old person will tell you – it really did sneak up on me.

I find myself staring at people on a crowded beach

thinking about young people. Doing absolutely nothing while waiting for an appointment, and not minding. I nearly fell asleep on the CT scan table because it was so comfortable. The world shrinks when you get old, and thank goodness for that, I say. Imagine the feeling of missing out, otherwise. Or the intensity of noise, and colour, and action.

After the trauma, heartbreak, drama and grief that you collect just by living this long, you understand that boredom is a treat to be savoured.

The small wonders still live large, and CF taught me those are the best ones. When I giggle with my son, it's heaven. Sitting up together in bed reading. A homegrown apricot eaten with the sun on my face really is the most joyous thing in the world. Look at that leaf, and see those snails climbing up the flower stalk while it's bending dangerously back to the ground. I wonder if they know they're doing that. Is it intentional?

I get complacent like anyone. It's hard to hold onto a feeling of aliveness all the time. I'm glad for a good kick in the grateful now and again. Getting changed into a gown ready for a recent bone density scan, I was babbling. I wish I could lose just that last tricky five kilos, and ha-ha measure me but no, I haven't grown much taller lately. The lovely white-haired radiographer told me her niece had CF too. 'Isn't it great how things have changed so much in CF?' I say. 'No,' she responds. 'She's sixteen. This one won't make old bones.'

I can't believe how young the doctors are, and they don't even seem to realise that this was a child-killer disease so recently.

Death is much better hidden behind the sheer bulk of medical technology now, but she's there, in the corner. I try to keep hold of the almost exquisite, enlivening feeling when you hold hands with death, the surest companion you'll ever have.

Notes

[1] Susan Sontag, *Illness as Metaphor*. New York: Farrar, Straus and Giroux, 1978, p.3.

A case for forgiveness – Goldie Goldbloom

On April 3rd, 2014, after not speaking to my father for over forty years, I call him. The telephone call is the culmination of a long process that began when I signed up for my first writing class in 2008. I live in Chicago. My father lives in Brisbane, Australia. I mess up the time difference. He is woken from his sleep at five in the morning. I can hear him floundering around, sneezing, blowing his nose. 'Who's that?' he asks. He sounds exactly the same as he does in my imagination. Angry.

'Goldie,' I say.

There is a long silence.

'Clairsie,' I say then, giving him my English name, the one he'd used for me in the 70s, just in case he didn't recognise my voice. The name I don't connect with myself anymore.

He begins to cry.

He cries for four minutes and thirty-seven seconds and then hangs up. I know that because my phone keeps a record of the length of the call.

I'm old now. I like being old because things that used to be sharp and painful have become blurry and soft. After forty years of his absence from my life, I've forgotten what my father looks like. I've lost the single photograph I had of him, a panoramic black and white snapshot from the 50s, a group of youths in leather jackets and white t-shirts and heavy boots on a train platform. Tattooed and grimacing, they are grouped around my father, their leader. His gang looks cool and dangerous, the first unofficial Hell's Angels gang in Albany, Western Australia; the Albany Angels. I have nothing to point to and say, yes, that's my dad. Each time I call my father, I hold the phone out to my children and put it on speaker for a few moments so they can hear his voice. It's all I have to give them.

I can't remember the simplest detail of his face, the colour of his eyes, the curl of his hair. I think it's his hands I remember when I picture thick fingers, freckled, sandy hair across the knuckles, heavily scarred by sea urchins, stonefish, cobblers, rays, jarrah floorboards, engine grease, fibreglass, knives. But they might be my grandfather's hands or my brother's. They might be a stranger's.

I try calling my dad a second time, a month after my first effort. I call later in the day when he has already been awake for a few hours, when he is out in his garage, tinkering with an engine.

'Who the bloody hell is this?' he asks.

'It's me, Dad,' I say. 'Goldie.'

Again the intake of breath. Again the catch in his throat. Again the long silence. But now he says, 'How are you, love?'

And that word, love, hangs in the echoing air between us, so very wrong, and yet somehow, so inexplicably right that I struggle for breath.

What do you say, after forty years, when you are asked how you are?

I'm good, Dad. On a lot of days, I'm good, but there's been some really terrible times too. Oh, and by the way, I know it's going to be a bit of a surprise, but you're a great-grandfather. I have eight children and the oldest is twenty-seven. The youngest is fourteen, two years older than I was when I stopped talking to you.

I'm fat now, a grandmother with a bun and no bra. I keep chickens. I teach writing at an Ivy League university. I am a novelist. My work is published around the world. I drive a tiny green Fiat and grow my own vegetables. I speak fluent Italian and Yiddish and Hebrew. Those Jewish languages will probably be a surprise to you. I'm a Chassidic Jew. Don't blame yourself for my conversion.

I don't say any of this.

After my father asks how I am, I am silent. I don't know how to compress forty years into a few sentences.

'Are you there?' he shouts. 'Fucking phone!'

A chain rattles, the sound familiar to me from weekends spent watching my father and brother take apart motors. He's quickly lowering the engine block into the carapace of a truck. A wrench hits a steel table. I wait for the sound of him chugging a bottle of beer. I let him bash the screen of his phone with his blunt fingers a couple of times, roaring, before I ask what he's fixing and it turns out he's repairing an old flatbed Toyota he bought at auction. It's winter in Australia and he's hoping it doesn't rain while he's outside. He's had a heart attack, no, he's had two heart attacks, and the latest one left him vulnerable to damp and raised blood pressure. But he'll never bloody take the medicine they give you at the doctor's because that's the stuff that really kills you. He uses a black salve that he keeps in a jar at the back of his fridge for the skin cancer that keeps on popping up on his ears and his neck and his chest. His buddies have all died as a result of butchering bloody doctors but he's going to make it to a hundred.

'How old *are* you, Dad?'

Until I stopped talking to him, he always said he was twenty-one. I have no clue how old he is now. If I have to guess, I'd say he's close to eighty.

'Twenty-one,' he says, and down the line comes the sharp snap of him popping out his front teeth and then clicking the bridge back into place and his self-satisfied hum at hoodwinking me yet again.

I want to laugh. It's like I am six or seven, sitting in the front of his ute, him pulling potatoes from my ears, pretending I haven't washed behind them well enough, cracking jokes, teasing his little girl, telling her he's twenty-one. He wasn't all bad. I know he wasn't. I know he wasn't.

'Happy twenty-first,' I say. 'I hope you had a bash.'

During the third or fourth call, my dad tells me about my great-grandfather, a man who left school when his own father became crippled in an accident. I've never heard this story before and I desperately want it to be true. As Dad talks, images rise in my mind: an emaciated man, my great-grandfather, in a top hat and tails – he's an undertaker – flogging the horses that draw the hearse in an effort to get back from the cemetery in time for a cricket match. The tall black hearse with its velvet drapes and etched glass windows swaying and creaking, the horses galloping along, their emu-feather headdresses blown backwards over their ears, dirt flying from under their hooves.

And later:

A story about teaching our puppy to piss on a peppermint tree. My father's leg raised. 'Like this!' he shouts. For a moment, we are not in Chicago and Brisbane. It's Western Australia. Flamborough Street, Doubleview. A tiny asbestos house on a hill near the sea. 1966. And as he recalls the gentle humour of that summer afternoon, I am reminded that once, he was my father in more than name.

These calls feel like some kind of healing for me. Afterwards, I sit outside on my verandah and listen to the birds and I am full of something approaching forgiveness.

For a man who didn't finish school, my father has a surprisingly deep love of language. *Gutless cowering. The knock on kinship. The irksome burden of trust.* The more I talk with him, the more I notice how similar we are. I am not sure how I feel about discovering that the gifts I most value in myself were all inherited from him: my imagination, my aesthetic sense, my obsession with books, my ability to write and draw well, my fascination with building and construction, my dark sense of humour, my love of cooking, my wordplay. Had I known this earlier, would I have suppressed these traits, grown more like my mother in an effort not to be like him?

In one exchange:

The cold steppes of electronic isolation. A gnat's tit of philosophical insight. Queynte of the decade. Beggars belief. Who are you bullshitting? Copping some stick.

Rubbishing. Oily praise. Intellectual chicanery. Punch to the face. Patently a fraud. Threadbare relationship. Steady downwards spiral. Haymakers. Sporto. Man up. Balls.

Queynte, it turns out, is an ancient and obsolete form of the word cunt. I write it into my little book of ancient and obsolete words, many of which I use on a daily basis. I include the word in a novel I am writing, delete it, put it back.

Before I cut him out of my life, my father liked to teach me things. He thought of himself as an educator. He taught me not to chew with my mouth open or let the spoon click against my teeth when I ate or to slurp soup and he taught me never, never, never to allow chewing gum or peanut paste or marshmallows (all American inventions) into my mouth. He taught me that people who drive automatic cars are lazy and that good drivers drive fast and talk fast when the police stop them. He taught me that words are delicious. He taught me that I had to finish everything on my plate even if it made me vomit. He taught me that if I did something I should do it well. He taught me that doing one thing well is not enough; I had to keep on learning new things all the time. He taught me 'I can't' really means, 'I don't want to.'

He taught me that the best bloody place in the entire universe was Western Australia and that the best part of Western Australia was the ocean and that the best part of the ocean were the fish and the best part of the fish was the eating. He taught me to tell the truth even if it meant I would be punished, because the punishment would be worse if I got caught telling a lie. He taught me to be on time and to write good letters and to thank people sincerely and to clean underneath my fingernails every day and to cut my toenails to the nub after softening them in a bath with eucalyptus leaves floating in the water. He taught me that if I brushed my teeth for five minutes three times a day I would never get false teeth, and that doctors and dentists are highway robbers who are out to fleece the common man and that if I was smart at all I would steer clear of them all the days of my life. He taught me to pay more for toothbrushes with boar bristles instead of that crap nylon that was probably scratching the enamel off my teeth so dentists could put more of his money in their pockets. Sugar rotted the teeth so I should never have lollies, but if I did, I should brush my teeth right away. He taught me to polish the brass buttons on his army jacket every week with a square of newspaper folded behind them so that the Brasso wouldn't end up on the fabric, and he taught me to give a hundred polishing strokes with a toothbrush before each button was finished and he taught me to clean the skirting boards on my hands and knees each Sunday with a toothbrush. He taught me to clean my shoes with a toothbrush dipped in linseed oil and he taught me to repaint my white sandals with a toothbrush dipped in whiting. He taught me to brush dirt over newly planted seeds with a toothbrush and he taught me to spatter green paint by rubbing a toothbrush over a bit of flyscreen and he taught me to scrub smashed flies off the walls with a toothbrush dipped in bleach. He taught me to pour hydrogen peroxide onto the bathroom tiles and then to clean the grout with a toothbrush. He taught me never to throw away toothbrushes and to categorise them as above the waist and below the waist. Above the waist could theoretically be cleaned enough to use on your teeth again in a pinch. Below the waist was permanently tainted. He taught me that gold teeth are the only kind of falsies to get if I was forced to replace something, though why that would happen if I was brushing three times a day he didn't know. He taught me it's a good idea to keep a spare above-the-waist toothbrush in your pocket. He taught me to push a piece of thread through the handle of the toothbrush and make it into a loop, so that if I got orange stuck in my teeth, I could get it out. He made me a small metal hook to dig other junk out from between my teeth. He taught me to brush my teeth for five minutes after every meal by standing behind me with a stopwatch in his hand. He taught me that farming is a mug's game. He taught me that the laws of society are hokum. He taught me that I could be a pirate if I robbed an institution but I couldn't touch anything that belonged to an individual. He taught me that if I took a hit off the nitrous oxygen canister in the shed at the farm that my voice would sound like Mickey Mouse's. He taught me that social homosexuality is a very real thing amongst Australian drinking men. He taught me to hate bullshit artists, even though he was one, and he taught me to hate cheats, though he was a cheat too. He taught me that fathers don't need to walk as slowly as their children. He taught me that men don't need to be kind to women. He taught me not to bellyache about things that didn't matter and not to whinge about the things that did unless I'd lost a hand or an eye. He taught me that Swan Lager is the best bloody beer on the planet and that you could drink ten bottles of beer and still drive home without hitting anything besides a few light poles and Blackie the cat. He taught me that drunks have wicked aim when they decide to throw something at you, and that when they can't find something small, it's okay to throw the drawer across the room. He taught me that leather is best when it comes time to discipline the children, but the back of a hand hurts worse than the palm. He taught me that children should be seen and not heard. He taught me that women's breasts are made to be worshipped and that bikinis are the best way to view a great variety of them. He taught me to play poker and Slippery Kate and Liar and Cheat. He taught me that blacks aren't as good as whites and that Jews aren't as clean as Christians and that Catholics aren't as intelligent as Protestants and that bloody damned Liberals didn't care about the working man as much as the Labor party and that intellectual snobs in their ivory towers didn't have half as much intelligence in their hands as the average yobbo laying bricks and that labrador retrievers were better than bull-mastiffs and that all dogs were better than all cats and that fishing was better than reading books and that dicks were better than tits and that men were smarter and faster and stronger and more ethical and kinder and more honest and more companionable and more parsimonious and less childish and more virile and infinitely more responsible and definitely more faithful than women.

I like to think these teachings are no longer me, that my father no longer lives inside my head and my heart. I like to imagine that I have somehow created myself *ex nihilo*. I am a Chassidic Jew. I live in Chicago. I have a cat, not a dog. I am terrified of taking something that isn't mine. Toothbrushes make me shudder. My kids rule the roost. I don't drink and I prefer women to men. The thing is, women's breasts are pretty nice. The ocean is the most beautiful thing on earth, particularly the Indian Ocean. I drive a manual car and laugh at people who drive automatics. I clean my bathroom tiles with peroxide. I still have never eaten a piece of chewing gum or a marshmallow. I am suspicious of academia. I am ashamed to be a racist.

When I was in my late forties, I enrolled in a writing class at Northwestern University. Despite having won an international fiction prize at the age of sixteen, despite being a freelance writer for decades, I'd decided that I was parochial, untalented and desperately in need of some marketable skills. I was the mother of eight children and spent hours every day cleaning my house with a toothbrush. I drove a fifteen-passenger van and my point of greatest pride was that I could park this mammoth with barely two inches to spare at each end on the streets of my crowded inner-city neighbourhood.

Every summer, I ran a spiritual community and an Outward Bound–style camp in the Kettle Moraine area of Wisconsin, where I'd designed, built and decorated all of the buildings, as well as played nurse to large groups of adolescent boys who came to me with things like wood ticks embedded in their scrotal sacs. I was also responsible for the laundry, which meant that I was washing, drying and folding about fifty loads a week. When I told my then husband that I wanted to take a night class, he snorted and asked, 'Who's going to watch the kids?'

My father, however, had taught me that if I did something,

I should do it well, so I signed up for a class with Fred Shafer, one of the real gems of the writing world. He is short and has snow-white hair like my father, but unlike my father, he speaks gently, with invitation, with compassion. His class lit me on fire. During that midwinter break, my family travelled to Florida and I wrote my first long literary story, 'The Road to Katherine'. It was a thinly fictionalised story about a road trip my family had taken when I was six in the far north-west of Australia, during which I was accidentally left at a remote water tank. When I read it over the phone to my brother, he laughed. 'It's all bloody true,' he said. 'You can't get credit for that at uni.'

For the first time since I was twelve, I'd begun – carefully, slowly, protectively – thinking about my father and his role in my life. I thought this analysis was going well but Fred very politely pointed out that the father in the story (no relation to mine of course. I was writing 'fiction') was a monster. 'Real people,' he said, 'aren't monsters.' I wanted to argue with him. They are, I wanted to say. Real people do such terrible things that their evil is beyond words. 'No-one believes in evil,' Fred said. 'It's boring. It's melodramatic. Try and find something likeable about this man.'

I almost quit the class because there was nothing I wanted to do less than find something likeable about my father. There was a reason I hadn't spoken to him in close to four decades! The character wasn't fiction and neither was the story. Dad wasn't a *melodramatic* figure to me. He was real.

But in the back of my mind, my father's voice saying that 'I can't' really means 'I don't want to'. After years of avoiding any thoughts about him, I suddenly wanted to understand my father and his psychology so my story would be accurate, clean, the best I could do. Ironically, that perfectionism was another inheritance from my father. I ended up studying psychology so I could avoid writing my father (or any human being) as a monster.

Being told to find my father's grace and then engaging in the slow process of revising the image I held of him set off a powerful transformation. At fifty, at last, I was no longer a child, terrified of bogeymen. I could call my father and imagine his pain rather than be ruled by my own. I was able to listen to his voice and let my children hear him too. Though I'd thought I was an adult when I got married, and when I had my first baby, and when I'd married off my son, and when I became a grandmother, it was only when I was able to imagine my father as a young and innocent boy that I truly became an adult.

Ignorance – Anne Aly

As the world was bidding farewell to the 70s, I was saying goodbye to my childhood. The year 1980 heralded a decade marked by extremes of unabated enthusiasm and apocalyptic dread.

It was the decade that saw the end of the Cold War, the assassinations of John Lennon and Anwar Sadat, Reaganism, Thatcherism, MTV, Madonna, the advent of the computer and electronic gaming, the end of the Berlin Wall, AIDS, Chernobyl, the *Challenger* disaster and bad fashion choices. Big hair, big shoulders, bold colours and bright lipstick weren't just the fashion faux pas of the 80s: they were the icons of a decade of excesses and the 'me first' generation.

I was about to enter the 80s as a teenager. The year I turned thirteen was my second year at Moorebank High School in Sydney's south-west. The school classified us into streams based on our academic ability. Academically, I had already proved myself as one of the better performers; I was in the 'A' stream, and could be assured that my classmates wouldn't tease me for being too smart. If there were cliques at our school, I was too young, or too preoccupied, to notice them. I had a good group of friends – both female and male – and was fast getting a reputation for being witty in class, though my teachers would probably have described me more as a smartypants.

There were still the occasional remarks about my dark skin by some kids, but as American pop culture saturated our TV screens with shows that made being black and/or ethnic cool and almost normal, my skin became something that made me 'exotic' – like an iguana or a giant penis-shaped plant that trapped live bugs and dissolved them in digestive fluid.

Most of the time I thought of myself as a fairly typical Aussie teenager, though I was acutely aware that there were things about me and my family that marked us as different, as 'new' Australians. We never went to the movies because my parents preferred to watch Arabic films at home, and they bought a video recorder as soon as they came on the market so that we never had any excuse to go to the movies. We never ate at restaurants because, as my father would say, 'Why should I pay someone to cook a meal for me when I can get your mother to do it for free?' We never took family trips to the country during school holidays or had lazy long weekends. We were never allowed to stay the night at a friend's house because, as my mother would say, 'Why would I let you sleep in a stranger's house? If your friends want to sleep, they can sleep here where we can keep an eye on you.' There were lots of things that we never did and that I wished we would do, because if we did those things, maybe that would make us more Australian.

As I grew out of my obsession with the Brady Bunch, finally coming to terms with the fact that Bobby Brady was never going to visit Australia, find me and make his TV parents adopt me, I began to imagine the quintessential Aussie family by observing those around me.

My dearest friend in my early teens, the closest thing I had to a sister after my real sister, was a girl who lived in our suburb. Tracey's family was one of the last to build in our street. She was a year younger than me and at first I was wary of her, thinking that we could not possibly have much in common. Physically, we had absolutely nothing in common. Tracey was petite, even for her age – like a child yet to catch up with her taller, broader, more physically developed peers. Her blonde hair framed her elfin face in what was a popular Princess Diana hairstyle of the day. I rarely noticed her slight awkwardness around other teens or the way she giggled shyly whenever she drew unwanted attention. She was, I thought, as beautiful as a delicate porcelain doll.

Some time during the summer of my thirteenth year, my body decided that it was time for me to grow up. I wasn't ready for round hips and breasts so big they strained against the fabric of my school uniform, causing the seams to split and the buttons to pop. They were just another feature that made me stand out as 'different': Anne Aly, the dark-skinned wog with the big boobs. I was so conscious of my gargantuan chest that I wore a school jumper over my uniform all through the year, even in the height of summer when the mercury would regularly reach forty degrees. While some teased her for her pre-pubescent, boy-like body, I envied Tracey her flat chest and slim hips. She glided effortlessly in her aeronautically engineered frame; I carried my burden of a body like the mythical Atlas.

Had I been left to judge a book by its cover, I probably would have thought of Tracey and her family as part of the ignorant and uneducated masses who believe Australia is in danger of being swamped by 'insert group here'. But stereotypes cut both ways, and ignorance is not something any of us are immune to if we live our lives separated by assumptions of difference, never having the opportunity to glimpse in others that which makes us frail, vulnerable and just human.

Quite by chance, Tracey and I ended up walking to school together one morning, and soon enough the twenty minute walk to and from school in each other's company became a ritual. We spent all our time after school, on weekends and on school holidays together. We tracked imaginary animal prints in the bushes, pretending that a giant feral cat was on the loose, and inventing wild new contraptions to capture it. We went jogging in the early mornings with our dogs and swimming in our backyard pools until late at night. When Tracey reached puberty, we shared the rites of passage into womanhood: make-up, our first concert (KISS), first heels and first *Cosmopolitan* centrefold (which didn't impress us much but provided us hours of laughter).

Tracey's dad was a big-bellied, beer-swilling, tattooed truck driver who looked an awful lot like Norm, the affable couch potato from the popular 'Life. Be in it.' television ads of the 70s. Her mum had regular perms, wore a bikini and laughed at her husband's lame jokes. Her younger brother was in the same year as my brother and they too became inseparable, often passing the time by having farting competitions, which both disgusted and amused us in equal measure. Our parents never became what I would call friends, but they were as civil as neighbours could be, and developed a mutual respect and affection for each other cultivated by their children's inseparability.

Every month, Tracey's family ate dinner at a restaurant. Not a dodgy café at the mall that served crusty egg and mayonnaise sandwiches and cold cups of tea, but a real, fancy restaurant: The Black Stump. My very first meal at a restaurant was with Tracey's family. I got to order real Australian food like steak and chips and salad, and garlic prawns and pasta. I joined her family at games nights where we all sat around the table playing cards or board games late into the night. I looked after their corgi when they went away to the country for long weekends.

Being around Tracey and her family made me feel … Australian. It was a feeling that had eluded me as long as I was constantly told that I wasn't Australian because I didn't, couldn't possibly, look Australian. Even now, the question 'Where are you from?' still makes me uncomfortable. I'm never too sure what to say: Sydney? Albury–Wodonga? Perth? WA? Egypt? I've learnt to gauge the meaning behind the question: whether it is out of innocent curiosity or something more sinister, like a poorly disguised attempt to segue to a debate about religion or the status of Muslim women. Not that I would shy away from a debate, but it gets kind of exhausting when all you want to do is enjoy your double chocolate sundae, or wrap up a polite conversation about the price of free-range eggs. I've also learnt not to roll my eyes with conspicuous exasperation when middle-aged men in suits ask me this question in the boardroom after I've just spent ten minutes speaking about the challenges to substantive equality, and developing social, economic and political participation in a democratic political system. Most of all, I've learnt not to focus so much on being different but to develop relationships based on commonalities: Tracey taught me that.

Teenagers lead secret lives, and I was no exception. When I was fourteen, I found a copy of Nancy Friday's book *My Mother/My Self: The Daughter's Search for Identity* in the library and it was as if I had been handed a whole new looking glass. Friday's assertion that 'The older I get ... the more of my mother I see in myself' scared the bejesus out of me. No way! No way was I ever going to be like my mother. I much preferred the other things Friday had to say about being a woman and how the ideals of womanhood passed down from mothers shackled their daughters.

I knew even back then what kind of woman I wanted to be, but I was incapable of comprehending just what it would take to be her: an independent, free-thinking, autonomous woman who took no shit – a disruptor. Sometimes I felt like my belly would swell and burst with all the anticipation of womanhood that was growing impatiently inside me. Sometimes I despaired that she would never see the light, destined to live her life, my life, curled up in the fetal position, tethered to an existence defined and dictated by men and mothers to save her from her own vulnerability.

I started reading everything I could get my hands on about feminism. I read Marilyn French's *The Women's Room* and warmed to its utterly despairing vision of femininity and marriage. From there I graduated to *The Feminine Mystique* and a sequence of novels that featured strong female protagonists. But it wasn't the Jane Eyres and the Jo Marches that I found appealing. As much as I discovered parts of myself in the writings of Western feminist authors of the 60s and 70s, I couldn't relate to the nineteenth-century heroines and the complexities of nineteenth-century social norms. I preferred reading stories about women who jumped out of planes or fought off monsters to all that nineteenth-century politeness.

I never spoke of these things. Not with my family, and not even with Tracey. I kept my thoughts private, retreating to my bedroom to read the books I kept hidden underneath my mattress. This was something that belonged to me and only me. I lived my life straddling two worlds. I could sing all the words to Madonna's 'Like a Virgin' (and know exactly what they meant) and convince my parents that I was their little angel who brought home good grades and didn't know what a penis was. I needed to do that to survive, avoiding an inevitable clash of cultures that threatened to implode my world. Anyone who has never had to negotiate two identities – often with conflicting expectations – cannot possibly understand just how adroit young women can be at slipping in and out of identities: princess, queen, slayer, diva, damsel.

Beyond the seclusion of my bedroom – where I meandered through pages exploring dangerous, exciting ideas – I lived a life dictated by expectations. As a normal teenager, I did normal teenage things. Tracey and I went to concerts and weekend rollerskating sessions and movies. We talked about boys and read teen magazines. Despite my secret reading habit, I formed my ideas about beauty and attractiveness from the glossy pages of *Dolly*, where pink-skinned pre-teens with shiny blonde hair and flat chests modelled leg warmers, polka dots and flared skirts.

Tracey's family moved away, and I lost touch with her before I finished high school. I thought about her often and wondered what happened to her and her brother, and the family that allowed me to do Australian things with them without judgement. I missed my childhood friend, my companion through the journey to womanhood who knew, more than anyone, how much I struggled to reconcile the me in my head with the me I saw in the mirror each morning: the me I knew others saw too.

Then, not so long ago, an email arrived in my inbox asking me if I was the same Anne Aly who had lived in Chipping Norton and had a brother named Sam. It was from Tracey's brother, who'd managed to track me down after seeing me interviewed on television. I had a thousand questions for him. What had become of my dear friend? Did Tracey become a vet like she always said she would? Marriage? Kids? Pets? What about horses? She always loved horses. And what of their parents? Were they still around?

Tracey's brother's reply came back immediately. He told me that he was sorry to hear my father had died, and that he and Tracey had always felt safe and loved at our house. But it was his next lines that stopped me cold. He wrote that their own father was in jail: he had been convicted as a paedophile, who had abused Tracey from when she was five until she was seventeen.

I cried for days. I cried for my friend and her lost innocence, and I cried for my own ignorance. I cried for the time I was seven years old and a stranger came into the bathroom with his pants down and his erection in his hand like a loaded gun, calling my name and trying to drag me close to him. I cried with relief and guilt for being spared the torment Tracey had endured. I cried because the new burden of my knowledge could never be as immense as the burden my friend had to carry all her life.

In retrospect, my greatest teenage challenges had revolved around straightening my curly hair, bleaching my upper lip and containing my burgeoning breasts. I can take some comfort in the fact that my family – the family I complained about constantly, that I wished could be more normal and less ethnic – gave Tracey and her brother a haven. I take comfort knowing that they felt loved and safe with us. And yet, the pettiness of my early teen obsessions still fills me with shame and hurts my heart. I'd had a secret life as a teenager, where I was working out the kind of woman I wanted to become. But it had never occurred to me, in my self-absorption, that Tracey might have had a secret life too.

Black boxes – Jeanine Leane

Whitefellas never can decide what kind of Blackfella they want. The bar is always shifting. But whatever kind of Blackfella they want – it's never me.

*Once, i*n the 1960s, when I was a child, they wanted us to look white, or at least whiter, and exhibit no obvious signs of our Blackness irrespective of what we may carry in our hearts. As long as they couldn't see it, we could gather, store and carry what we wanted on the inside. They didn't want us speaking language either – only English, the language of power. But English always did a different dance when it rolled off our tongue – one that was a bit out of step with the power-dance. Back *then*, they said we should try and succeed in western education, learn their culture, their history, and then we'd get ahead, and move to cities too, because they are the heartland of high white culture.

Now, we get to the twenty-first century and they want us to look Black – the blacker the better. Any obvious signs of culture worn externally are great. If you come from a former mission, or a remote community – that's of great interest now, to whitefellas. If you came through an alternative access program especially designed for Indigenous people post-1980 – even better. And if you are young and meet all the criteria above, you'll be a prize for any White Department of History or Anthropology at a university because it will mean that whitefellas didn't really get rid of all the *real ones* – they saved some of us for this current exhibit. They've decided they like grassroots Aborigines now – as long as the grass is growing on the right side of the fence.

I am middle-aged, have olive skin, and was not born at a remote community or on an archaeological site that whitefellas might make a film or write a book about. My family escaped the mission system and I was fortunate enough not to be stolen. I cannot speak any Aboriginal language, nor do I pretend to. While weathering many uninformed, ignorant and sometimes blatantly racist comments from both teachers and peers, I mastered the western education system through the 60s and 70s, gaining outstanding results in English literature and European history – even getting a prize from my school and two nice bright stars on my brand new High School Certificate because I scored in the top ten per cent of the state.

I was encouraged to 'go out into the world' by my Aunties – they worked hard to put me though school, convincing and cajoling me all the way through some difficult times on the strength of the hope that my generation would make a difference. So, I went to university with the whitestream because I got in too, along with all the other first-generation working class kids in the late 70s and early 80s who got there – thank you, Gough Whitlam. We made many of our professors cringe and squirm because most of them were meeting the plebs for the first time.

I made it. By the time I graduated, I was speaking and reading English better than the average whitefella. At school and, later, university, I got used to being outside the square. Back then I was often the only Aboriginal student in the class and I was never like the ones in the textbooks or the ones some of my lecturers had done PhDs on. I was young and easily dismissed as inauthentic in those days – I was obviously delusional, as I quite clearly exhibited none of the necessary outward displays of cultural reference points.

'Aboriginal descent!' one of my lecturers corrected me when I told her after the lecture (or tried) that I was Wiradjuri from the Murrumbidgee River. She had written a book on Aborigines for all first-year history students.

'Des-cent!' She was adamant. 'The area was colonised so early that the Wiradjuri clans were cleared out by the 1880s.'

My family wasn't 'cleared out' – neither were the other Wiradjuri families who lived and worked around the Tumut and Gundagai areas. But we weren't in the textbook either.

Teaching high school in Canberra through the 80s was no different. There were no boxes to tick back then. If colleagues asked about my cultural background at all it was usually: 'Are you Italian, Spanish – French maybe?'

'No, I have no European ancestry at all. I'm Aboriginal.'

'Oh you don't look it! Not both your parents?'

'My father was Irish.'

'Well, why don't you say you're half Irish?'

'Because I didn't really know him – it was my mother's family who influenced my life.'

Noses wrinkled, eyes narrowed, brows rose – I read disbelief on their faces. 'But you're not really!' Some would add: 'Not fully.' Others just gave me the blank two hundred year stare of un-seeing before they walked away.

So that was the 80s – outside the box and inauthentic. For the first half of the 90s, I was having babies and raising children. It was towards the end of the 90s when I was enrolling my children in local schools and looking to return to the workforce myself that the box first appeared. Since then it has been around with a vengeance. And while life outside the metaphorical box that existed in the heads of white academics meant inauthenticity, I was about to learn about a new way of life at the dawn of the twenty-first century: life inside the box.

Quite by accident I landed a job in the tertiary sector in 2000 in an Indigenous Higher Education Centre. I had to fill in a form for the new Department of Education when I was applying to go back into the workforce. There was a box that simply asked: *Are you Aboriginal?* And I ticked it.

It might seem like a small box – a couple of millimeters perhaps – you'd think at first you'd barely fit a tick or a cross within its boundaries. Yet once inside, with just one flick of a pen, you're trapped forever. Within this tiny space is the mindset of settler Australia: the perceptions, permissions, expectations and limitations of what Blackness is to Whiteness in twenty-first century.

Each straight-lined side is as inflexible as a cell wall – it's impossible to escape this square. The empty expanse between the right angles is Arctic tundra – a white wasteland; and, you'll wonder, as I do, how something that once looked so small could become such an unbridgeable chasm, an unsurpassable gap. A blackfella like me can spend their whole life running round in one of those black boxes. Those fine black lines that seem so flimsy are impenetrable. But I didn't know that then, the first time I ticked that box.

The university was 'Indigenising' its space and embedding Indigenous perspectives across the curriculum – this is what I was told as the reason for my name being put forward as a qualified secondary teacher who was Aboriginal. Emerging back into the workforce after ten years of motherhood to the brave new world of the twenty-first century, I was officially Aboriginal, not just 'part' or 'descent', but inside a black box now.

'The university is transitioning,' the dean told me when I signed the contract after I ticked the box. 'Your challenge,' he went on, 'will be to prepare Indigenous students in pre-tertiary programs for tertiary entry.'

But my real challenge was educating the whitestream. The average settler academic knew next to nothing about twenty-first century Aboriginality. Preparing students who are already bright, keen, enthusiastic and most of all, fully cognisant of the hard road our ancestors walked and the battles fought to get us the right to equal education in the first place, was easy. The real challenge was explaining behind the scenes to whitestream teachers why we all look the way we do now – which is very different to what is expected; why we speak the way we speak – mainly Aboriginal English; why we live where we live – mainly in cities and larger regional centres. Why don't we all speak a language? Why can't we all tell a 'Dreamtime story', as the whitefellas call our creation stories? Why do some of us not want to study ourselves, anthropologically, historically or sociologically, in the white academy?

The demands of that small box became vast. Many of my white colleagues spent a good deal of time lamenting the 'loss of our traditional culture' when our contemporary culture was all around – we simultaneously confused, confounded, surprised and disappointed the majority of our white colleagues.

I was the most disappointing of all. I don't play sport or even follow it; I hate rugby league and its sanctioned violence, hype, crowds and cheerleaders; I can dance, but only ballet or to 70s and 80s dance music; I play some instruments, but none of them typically Aboriginal; I can't explain the meaning of a central desert songline, nor should I try without proper knowledge; I don't have *the* Aboriginal word for every place in Australia; and I don't have the answer for the 'Aboriginal problems' that my colleagues saw and frequently expressed concern about in the media.

I found myself in an institutional time-warp where a great deal of energy was spent with questions and concern about the lost past and the problematic, dysfunctional present that they know is out there – the stuff inside the box we tick that makes the whitefella on the other side of the desk, an authority on you.

In 2002, I was encouraged by a non-Indigenous colleague to write and present a research paper at an Indigenous Researchers Forum in Perth. Their idea was that I would present something on my work in Indigenous education – working with Indigenous people in pre-tertiary programs and supporting students through undergraduate degrees – helping my people swim up the whitestream.

But I wanted to swim back down the whitestream of consciousness to the genesis of these literary representations of us that still make waves further upstream in the present; those that still batter us and leave many of us stranded. And then, swim back up that stream again to take the journey through the evolution of us in the white literary imagination – a lonely journey of discovery where I would see my self netted many times before I arrived back in the whirlpool of the present where the representations are still coming.

'A bit out of the box!' said my colleague, when I showed them the paper. 'Well-written of course, but not really to do with Indigenous education and what you're doing.'

The aim of the forum was to bring together the research and experiences of Indigenous people working in universities with the view to forming networks, encouraging further Indigenous-led research and entry into higher degrees by research. Blackfellas with higher degrees by research were scarce as hen's teeth in the early 2000s and for the most part the professors and senior researchers were whitefellas who were working with blackfellas to 'indigenise the curriculum'.

For the most part, my colleague back in Canberra was right. The topic of my paper was too outside the box.

'Commendable scholarship,' said one academic with a long track record of working with Aboriginal anthropology and a more recent one of working with the descendants of the subjects of that fieldwork, 'but most Aboriginal students don't study literature in my experience – not beyond high school anyway, so would they really be affected by what authors said about them last century?'

'Impressive knowledge of Australian literature, but I can't see how this kind of research relates to the wider Indigenous community at all,' said another, more dismissively.

But there was one person who got it; someone who had spent a great deal of his life under the influence of the 'findings' and representations of an 1861 Cambridge expedition to his part of the world to observe 'primitive people in their natural state'. On this day the spirits were with me and I had the good luck to find one of the few

Indigenous professors among us – the only person present who had a background in humanities. And it only takes one person to believe in you.

I left that university thinking about the enduring legacies of representation: the textbooks I wasn't in; the anthropologists, archaeologists and historians that didn't study me; the authors who wrote about *the Aborigine*. With those thoughts in mind, I walked almost accidentally into a PhD with the representations of us in the settler imagination still on my mind.

I finished my PhD when I was fifty. I was coming to the end of a fixed-term contract and about to relocate to New York from Australia. My PhD focused on whitefellas' obsession with blackfellas in literature. I called it literary history and cultural literacy – how do you read a book that whitefellas wrote about blackfellas that really says more about whitefellas?

Pretty much everyone except my Indigenous supervisor thought it was unusual, but I was obsessed with Katharine Susannah Prichard, Xavier Herbert, Patrick White and a long line-up of nationally and internationally acclaimed authors who depicted Aboriginal characters, playing literary chess with blackfellas and our stories – using us as pawns in their chequerboard nation. These people are, after all, part of the reason why whitefellas are 'experts' on Aborigines.

'*Really*?' my son's primary school teacher said when she asked about my doctorate. 'Patrick White – not something Indigenous?'

She didn't wait for my explanation.

I weathered lots of questions about my PhD because deconstructing the representations absorbed me – and I thought someone might want to read about cultural literacy sometime.

Others enquired why I was so preoccupied with the dead white ghosts.

'Nobody reads them anymore do they? – except maybe a handful of academics; they don't have much bearing on the lives of the average person.'

Or: 'They're not really that influential anymore are they – the dead white literati?'

Dead or alive, their works still speak in Australian curricula. Only whitefellas think that the dead cannot speak.

I was in New York in the northern summer of 2011, excited with my brand new PhD, when I fronted up to a New York University on the recommendation of an Australian scholar from home. I was hopeful as I made my way through Alphabet City up the gridded, numbered streets past avenues D, C, B and A, from the Lower East Side to the West Village. It was a sunny day and I paused under the shadow of the victory arch outside Washington Square Park before I headed down Fifth for my interview at the Center for Australian Indigenous Studies.

I was going to meet two professors there, Zara and Zed, a husband and wife team – both of whom I was told had a long-term relationship with Australian Aboriginal people. One had spent time in Australia researching Indigenous art practices and the other through cinema, working with Indigenous and non-Indigenous Australian filmmakers to produce films on Aboriginal culture.

Did I think because I had a PhD now I'd be dealing with a different mindset? Did I think because the centre had the word 'Indigenous' as part of its branding that it might be a haven of enlightenment – a centre of twenty-first century epiphanies? I suffer from chronic incurable optimism.

Professors Zed and Zara had expressed an interest to their colleague in Australia about the possibility of providing space in their department for research and to network with the handful of Australian blackfellas living in New York and other scholars working in the field. I thought it might be a good opportunity to find a space to finish the research fellowship in a university environment and meet other people.

So I made my way to the top of the vertical campus and down a long corridor through some plush-looking decor with a vast array of Aboriginal canvases adorning the walls. As I made my way past the smorgasbord of traditional Aboriginal art from all over my Country I began to hear alarm bells in my head. But my unyielding optimism drowned them out.

I opened the door at the end of the corridor where a silver-haired, spectacled man sat absorbed in paperwork. I stood for a moment in the doorway – I was a little early but thought that might look impressive. He didn't look up so I knocked.

'Yes,' he said still fixated on the papers before him.

'I'm Jeanine,' I said, stepping in, hand extended.

'Oh,' he stepped out from behind his desk and met my handshake, 'from Aus-tra-lia.' He stared intently and continued to shake.

'Yes, my friend and colleague, Luke from the Research Institute rec–'

'*Ahhh...*' he let go of my hand, turned and picked up the papers from his desk, 'you mean the Wirr ... Wir-rid-jer-ee woman from the Murrum ... Murrum-bid-gee River near Gundag ...'

'Yes,' I said, coming to his rescue, 'that's me, the Wiradjuri woman from the Murrumbidgee River near Gundagai.'

Professor Zed glanced at his papers and back at me again – faint furrows rippled across his brow. 'Take a seat, please,' he gestured to the vacant chair and resumed his place on the other side of the desk. He waved at the pile of papers he'd been reading and placed them in front of him, 'Zara will be here in a minute. We've just been reading about you.' He looked back at the papers. 'An impressive PhD indeed – amazing engagement with the settler canon too ... the title though, *Tracking*, led me to believe that it was something completely diff–'

'Hello!' beamed a voice from behind.

'Oh ... Zara,' Zed looked up at the smiling woman carrying coffee and doughnuts, 'this is Jeanine.'

Zara placed the cardboard tray on Zed's desk. 'Lovely to meet you – Zed and I were just looking over your research folio.' She handed me a coffee. 'Impressive – lots of um ... interesting literary analysis – a little different from what we thought though,' she pursed her lips, 'I expected to read something about trekking and tracking through your country.' She was still smiling, but it was becoming blank – bemused.

'Yes,' Zed came to her rescue, 'I was thinking I was going to encounter the game and the traditional gathering and ...'

'Well, no actually,' I jumped in, 'it's a reference to a traditional practice but it was me tracking whitefellas representing us in national literature.'

Zara sat back on her chair – her brow puckered. Zed stared blankly across the desk. I tried again.

'It's metaphorical – I used tracking the way it was explained to me by my Nanna as a tool of literary analysis to track the whitefellas' consciousness of us in the national narrative.'

Silence. I pushed on. 'Gathering too – it's a traditional practice carried out by women and I'm looking at how that translates to writing and ...' I trailed off. Zara was staring out the window behind me. Zed was looking back over the pages in front of him. *The boxes* – those neat, tiny white squares.

They told me my work didn't 'quite fit' with what they were doing at the moment, but that they had my details, and maybe there would be a space for me a little later in the year. They would let me know if the situation changed.

I walked out and the sun was still shining. I wandered across Washington Square Park to where the old Black guys play chess in the corner with tourists for money and the chance to talk. After only a month in New York they already knew me. I gravitated there a few days a week with my notebook or my laptop to write. I made them laugh because I couldn't play chess and told them stories about Australia. They liked stories about blackfellas from home. I gave them all lapel pins of the Aboriginal flag that I brought with me. They wore them on their baseball caps and liked to point them out to me when I stopped by. They got it when I explained that the black on the top of the red is our people on the land even though we don't all look black on the outside. On that day, I sat in the sun with them and watched them move big plastic pawns across black and white squares.

I dream of a future where the space in which you sign your life away for whitefellas is a soft-sided circle – something not so angular and rigid that changes the shape of the expectation. I dream of a brave new Australia where my children can rock up to an interview where the only expectation will be that they are qualified to do the job they are applying for, and they will not have to spend time qualifying why they don't meet the boxed expectation of the interviewer in the first place.

I dream on – outside the box.

Memories that shaped me – Tracey Arnich

I was born in Tasmania from a long line of tough women of convict heritage. They were strong and powerful in their love. From an ancestral and present point of view, the women in my family are the glue that binds us together.

In the nineteenth century, two of my ancestors were deported to Tasmania. One brother owned a hat, a man tried to steal it and both brothers fought him. The man died and the brothers were deported, one to Maria Island, the other to Norfolk Island. The brother that was sent to Norfolk Island had a wife who refused to abandon her husband and boarded the ship as a free settler to follow him. She was the first white female to own farmland on Norfolk Island, and her husband was billeted to her.

At the age of sixteen, my mother brought me into the world. My father was a handsome man who loved to gamble, womanise and create debts. He was a carpenter and not considered a good prospect because of his past; he'd been to jail.

Mum's family wanted her to terminate her pregnancy, but she refused and married instead. She gave birth to my brother twelve months after me, and my sister quickly followed.

Mum and Dad separated when I was six. At the time I was in hospital having my tonsils out. When I left hospital,

I stayed with Dad. I don't remember going with him, I just remember I didn't want to leave him and my golden labrador, Chick the chicken killer. Mum left with my siblings. I don't recall much about living with Dad, but I remember the day Mum came and took me away from him.

We moved to a hovel of a house, built in a dug-out pit on the side of Mount Lyell, the back of the house sunk in clay. We had no furniture except an old meat safe in the kitchen and a mattress on the floor. There was no hot water; we had a copper outside that heated water for the bath, alongside an old laundry mangle.

Mum had two jobs and we didn't see her often. As the oldest, I'd look after my siblings, cook and care for them. I had a brilliant imagination and would constantly invent games and stories. We ran free and wild, the bush was our backyard, and the iridescent quick sand of the Queen River was our playground.

Mum's second relationship was with a South African. He was a violent man. I remember the beatings we got from playing Tarzan by swinging on the curtains and breaking them. When that relationship dissolved, I was happy, because it meant we weren't going to South Africa where there was apartheid and I would be unable to play with whoever I chose, black or white.

Once, Mum let our dad visit. He took us shopping and bought us giant pandas – mine was white and blue. I recall my siblings and I in his car, driving to the top of a hill in the dark. We were hungry, upset and afraid. Dad had a gun. He phoned my Mum and told her we wouldn't see her again. I remember a police officer holding my father at gunpoint, and then we were returned to Mum.

We moved to Hobart and rented a two-storey house. They were happy days, just Mum and us kids. We each had a room on the top floor with sloping walls. We were so excited to have our own rooms, but it didn't last. Mum took in a lady as a boarder to help pay the rent. Then my brother got very sick and needed urgent heart surgery in Melbourne. Mum had to leave me and my sister in the care of the boarder while she went with my brother; she had no-one else. They were gone a long time, and the boarder took away our rooms before they returned.

Then my mother met the man who would become my stepfather. He was Croatian. At first, he seemed wonderful. Mum went to university, and then worked for the attorney-general's office. She grew her own fruit and vegies and bought offcuts of meat to make soup.

My siblings and I formed a group of friends, sometimes two, sometimes four, so we were the Famous Five or the Secret Seven, and we would go on adventures picking blackberries and stealing cabbage leaves, hiding under the house to eat them. We used to trade blackberries with an elderly lady who would let us play in the historical courthouse where she lived. Once she went on holiday but didn't tell us and we thought she'd been murdered and called the police. The old building had a moat, cellars and prison cells underneath.

At Christmas, Mum would give us our year's supply of clothes and a few toys. She'd buy throughout the year and store it all in a suitcase under her bed. She'd make us clothes. One year I got a mini sewing machine, which I hated. Another year I got a typewriter and the others got bikes. One year she went out with my stepfather, and we snuck into her room and unwrapped our presents (I was the only one who could read the tags) and played with them. That year we didn't get anything – Mum said she gave our presents to an orphanage.

My great-grandmother had given Mum a deposit to buy a Housing Department house, which we lived in with my stepfather. Mum laid new carpets and wallpaper. There was an open fire in the lounge room, and one cold night, when we were fast asleep tucked in our beds, a spark jumped over the fire screen and ignited Mum's autumn leaf–patterned couch. Workmen from an early bus broke down our door, and we escaped, standing across the road, watching everything we owned disappear, engulfed by flames.

I felt free.

My stepfather was a house painter who did not like to work much. He preferred to drink. He was a giant of a man, a volatile bully who dealt out emotional and physical abuse. Once he didn't speak to me for a whole year; it was a hard thing to handle. During this time, my little brother, his son, was born. The household fell silent when his car entered the driveway. We'd wait for him to come in the door and look at his face:

How are his eyes today?
Fear
Silence

He ate his dinner at his own separate table. If he didn't like what was on the plate, he turned it into a flying saucer –

Whoosh!

Plate flying; food smashed up the wall. One of us would be singled out to clean it and the others couldn't help, we'd be bashed if we did. He liked to hit us with a belt, using the buckle end. My sister and I tried not to cry, and would laugh at him instead, refusing to give in.

It was very bad for a long time. One night I was standing at the kitchen sink. He was belting Mum; she grabbed my hair to stop herself from falling. I went down too.

Panic!

Curled on the floor

Mum's blood on the lino, him kicking her in the guts, her face his football

I got up, crept away, gathered my brothers and sister, and we quietly climbed out a window and ran to a safe house.

I wanted to die at that point, but I couldn't leave my brothers, sister and Mum. The police used to patrol our house, the neighbours knew but no-one did anything. Mum didn't have the option to escape; he always knew where we were. She went to a woman's shelter once. When she came back to get us, he'd nailed up the windows and doors, with us inside. And so we stayed, and the violence continued.

My father used to send me books with my name inscribed inside, but none for my siblings, his son and daughter. Sometimes I'd cross out my name and write in theirs, so they had something from him as well. When I was nine, he came to visit from Queensland. He took us out and bought me a radio. Then he took me to a field where there was a pony, and he told me it was mine. I was so excited. But it was a lie. I refused to believe my mum when she told me. So, she took me to meet the pony's owner.

Dad said he wanted me to live with him in Queensland. Mum said if I went with him, I could never return to live with her. I saw my father three times in my life after that.

The violence escalated with my stepfather. I wanted to sedate the giant; we were safe when he slept. Mum and I crushed valium tablets into powder, adding it to his salad. I thought I'd become a murderess, just to make it stop. One day I tried something that foamed up green in his coffee and I just got it down the sink before he saw it.

He flew to Croatia for his mother's funeral. We packed up the house overnight.

Escape! No goodbye to friends; tell no-one!
Get on the plane!
Change your name!

Arriving in Perth dressed in my woollies was a shock. It was as if I'd landed on another planet; the weather was so hot and sweltering. The trees were different, alien to me. There was no real dirt, just sand. The absence of gutters surprised me. We drove for what seemed an eternity, and arrived at Scarborough Beach. The ocean was extraordinary. I was so happy to be alive with my family, but I missed my Tasmanian mountains and clear seas.

I lived a colourful existence as a young woman in Perth; I went to art school, worked at various pubs, and dated a few people before I met the father of my son. He was a taxi driver and I met him by dialling the cab companies to see who was quickest to respond. When he left Perth for Sydney, I decided to follow, so I hitchhiked across the Nullarbor with my cat in search of him.

I arrived in Sydney with ten dollars to my name; I met an old friend on the street who said I could sleep on his couch for fifty dollars a week. I dropped my cat and bag there and went out to buy a sandwich. I overheard two girls talking, one asking the other if she could do her pub shift that night, but she couldn't. I said I could, and they told me to go to a leather shop on Oxford Street and ask for Glenys.

I worked that night at a pub and made about a hundred and fifty dollars in tips and wages. Later I caught a cab into Kings Cross and ended up at a nightclub. I asked for work and started then and there as a drinks waitress. I took my first drink order to the bar and the person that served me was the love I had followed to Sydney.

I got a job managing a club in the Cross, downstairs from my partner's flat. I recall hanging Chinese paper lanterns in the windows of his bedroom and lighting candles in them, looking out at the night workers. Ours was also a night life, working in clubs, eyes adjusting to morning, sleeping at noon.

After a year or so we moved to a share house in Auburn. It was a quieter lifestyle; on our weekends we'd watch *Rage* and David Attenborough videos. I got a job working at an auction house, valuing antiques, and I got my partner a job working in their vehicle yard.

We came back to Perth one Christmas on a Greyhound bus, and bought a Morris Minor to drive back to Sydney. Somewhere on the Nullarbor it started overheating. We picked up a young hitchhiker who had no water. We returned him to his Adelaide family, but the Morris was struggling and we were stranded.

We sold the Morris, but had very little money, not enough to get to Sydney. We went into a pub and I started playing the pokies, winning enough to feed us. I began talking with a man who part-owned the 4WD shop over the road from the pub. He said we could stay in his shop if we cleaned up the workshop area. We slept in a different 4WD every night, it was quite romantic, and I learned to drink beer, as Adelaide water was undrinkable.

One day I won a coin toss and the prize was the chance to buy a 1962 Datsun Bluebird ute, pulled from a paddock, for four hundred and fifty dollars, which we did. So, workshop cleaned, we drove back to Sydney.

We had many adventures in the ute. It had great big fenders and had to be hand-cranked to start. We slept in the back with a carpet of stars above us. If it rained we put a tarp over the top. The car moved slowly and bits of it fell off along the way. They were happy days, no radio and a partner who sang Johnny Cash.

I fell pregnant when I was twenty-seven, but I lost the baby. That loss was hard. We went like rabbits till I got pregnant again. We quit auctions and flew back to Perth for the birth.

My beautiful son was induced at thirty-seven weeks because the doctors thought his heart rate was too low. He was so tiny, perfect, looking like a wise crinkled old man. I could cradle him in my forearm. I could dress him in doll's clothes.

We lived in a cheap house in Lathlain, and I didn't know anyone. I think I had postnatal depression, but it wasn't talked about then. I developed mastitis; I had Incredible Hulk boobs, huge and deep blue veins. I lost my milk and really had to work to get it back. But I did.

I tried to find my father when my son was born. That's when I discovered he died of a punctured spleen under suspicious circumstances, when I was about sixteen. He was left by the side of the road; I have the newspaper clippings. I was deeply saddened because I would have liked him to meet my child.

My partner and I separated when our son was about two. Even though our relationship had dissolved, we remained united in raising our son. After we separated, my son and I moved to a house closer to the heart of the city. I started meditating and practicing tai chi, reiki and chi gong. I joined a spiritual group that met at a church in Subiaco.

I met my daughter's father in a nightclub. He was backpacking through Australia. We soon moved in together and then set up a co-op that sold antiques and collectables, but he cheated on me. I packed his bags, rang the woman he was cheating with and told her to come and get him. I deserved more.

We dissolved the co-op and he moved back to his home country, but by then I was already pregnant with his child, my beautiful daughter. I got a job in the markets while I was pregnant, and I went back to work at the markets the day after her birth; I felt fantastic. She was born a strong big baby, inside her placenta, which was a heart-shaped pouch.

I spent ten years selling clothing and gifts at the markets, firstly for someone else and then for my own business. There was a real sense of community in the markets. My children were known by all the stall holders. This was an extremely happy time in my life. The markets were only open three days a week which allowed me to have a very active role in my children's schooling; I cooked for the canteen, taught art classes and ran book fairs.

Then the markets closed due to redevelopment, and I started working as a florist. This has been my employment ever since. I work with colours, scents and textures, helping people celebrate their special moments in life.

My mother lost her fight with cancer few years ago. My sister and I took turns looking after her in her last days. It was quick and it was heart-breaking. I made Mum's funeral casket beautiful, covered in her favourite flowers, a celebration of her difficult life, and her strength.

Then when my beloved cat died after twenty-one years, I cried an ocean of tears.

My mother instilled strong family bonds in her children and we have all remained close. My children are also close; to me, to each other and to the other siblings they both now have.

I look back on my life and I am filled with gratitude because I have been given hope, mercy and compassion.

I am grounded, resilient and ready, moving into my new self as I age, experiencing menopause, embracing my curves, greying hair, glasses. I feel I will someday return to Tasmania. But in the meantime, I try and live my life in the best way I can, helping others when they need it, bringing the strength of my past into the present; being strong.

Work in progress – Maria Scoda

Sex, love, death, betrayal, tragedy, heartache, letting go. There is nothing that can't be spoken about in my rooms. I am a vault, a safe place where my clients can share their vulnerabilities and talk about the things that are troubling them. Sometimes I can help and sometimes all I can do is bear witness to their story. I don't have a little pill to give them, or a magic wand to take away the pain, not for my clients and not for myself. I listen, I comfort, I reassure and I help process. I do whatever I can, but there is no panacea.

I learnt to swim when I was five. My mother walked with my brother and me half an hour each way to take us to the public pool for lessons. I loved the feeling of her wrapping me up in a big soft towel after getting out of the water.

Seven years old and I'm in the squad. One, two, three, breathe. One, two, three, breathe. My heart pounding and my legs shaking. Struggling to stay afloat, I reach over to my right and hold onto the side of the pool. Resting my head on my arm, I try to catch my breath. I hate swimming in the rain but apparently it makes you stronger. Not me though, I just feel cold and shiver uncontrollably. Looking up at the stall, I wave, trying to get my mother's attention but it's Mr Brown, my coach, who notices me as he paces up and down the pool. He slaps my fingers with his thong until I let go and start swimming again. My eyes are focused on the black line below me. Keep going or drown – that's what I learnt in that pool.

In years to come, the pool becomes a place where I unwind and take some time for myself. It is a place where I feel free. All I can hear is the sound of my breath as if it is amplified in a large empty room. It is so deep and so rhythmic that it often sounds like a purr.

The human condition can be complicated, but we're not overly mysterious in our desire for love, peace and purpose in life. Feeling as though we don't matter can be a painful thing.

My father and mother emigrated from Italy, but at different times and from different places. They met in Marrickville and only knew each other for three months before they married. 'We moved to Bankstown, twenty minutes further west, for our honeymoon,' Dad joked. That's where I grew up in the 60s: a working class suburb with streets lined with fibro houses and old station wagons. My brothers and I played cricket, climbed trees and rode our bikes up and down the street. We only went in when our mother called us for dinner. My mother's family in Italy were poor. They got what they needed from simple things. I remember her telling me how when she was young she pretended that a rock was her doll. 'I threw it up in the air one time and on the way down, it hit me on the head,' she laughed. 'I bled so much, and I still have the scar.'

My parents worked hard and did what they could to assimilate, and for the most part, things were good for us. But there were times when we were reminded that we didn't quite fit, when people called us wogs or made fun of my name. By the time I was a young adult that was less of an issue. My Italian heritage seemed to have become more mainstream, part of the Australian norm.

Growing up, there was a degree of familiarity hanging around non-Anglo Australians, but I was at odds with some of the southern Mediterranean old-world views that many of the migrant diaspora subscribed to. It was hard to ignore the unspoken code that revealed itself when I met others from similar backgrounds, which I thought of as the ethnic nod. It went something like this: *you should know better, good girls don't go out late at night, or go to places where there are boys, or smoke. And they certainly don't move out of home or have sex until they're married.* But I wasn't a good girl – and as an older teenager I distanced myself from those values as much as possible.

I met one of my best friends at a drama class in my twenties. She mattered to me, still does. After our first class we went to the pub and sat at the bar and talked until the early hours of the morning. We shared an interest in books, the arts, coffee and vodka. The world was ours but I had no idea where I fitted in, or if in fact I did. I paid a karmic astrologer a hundred dollars to see if she could shed any light on things, and she said that in my previous life I roamed freely in the bush alone with no commitments, and that my purpose in this life was to build a meaningful relationship and work–life balance. That was encouraging, but I didn't know how to make that happen, and I had even less confidence in myself that I could.

I was an ordinary kid who asked a lot of questions, most of them beginning *but why?* – much to the annoyance of my parents. I sang and danced (badly) and played hopscotch, and loved our goldfish and grey tabby cat. School was a place I enjoyed, and I had many friends. I remember sitting cross-legged and playing with my kindergarten teacher's brown suede shoes as she told a story to the class. I was fascinated that they changed colour from dark to light brown as I rubbed them. She helped us learn the alphabet and to write; she asked us what we wanted to be when we grew up – as if we could do or be anything we wanted in that far away time of being an adult.

I failed my high school certificate. For a long time, I had excelled at school, but in my final two years as my home life became less happy and more complicated, I lost interest and my grades plummeted. I went from being a well-behaved child to an argumentative and defiant teenager, lacking confidence and confused about who I was and where I belonged in the world. Lost in my unproductive thoughts, I found myself regularly seeking the comfort and familiarity of the pool.

I haven't always been a psychologist. For a few years after I finished high school I went to secretarial college, but I never finished the course. I couldn't really type or take shorthand but I found I was particularly good at organising people and writing up presentations. I didn't mind working all night if I had to, or picking up a new shirt for my boss. When you're young and hopeful, any learning is good.

'You'll never be a secretary,' I remember my lecturer insisting just before she kicked me out of the course. 'You can't type and you don't look like a secretary. Can't you see how nicely all the other girls dress?' She was right; I had no interest in wearing pencil skirts, uncomfortable shoes or lipstick, but it still stung.

I felt like I was going to drown, but I pushed on. After leaving college I went through a couple of unskilled office jobs, which I quit because I found sitting in small dingy offices, answering the occasional phone call, soul-destroying. One of them ended for other reasons: I met a man one night through friends, and he offered me work at his law firm. I was excited about this job as it was an opportunity to build my secretarial skills, but within days he started asking me out and I believe it was my ongoing rejection of his sexual advances that got me fired within a few weeks.

I was only nineteen years old but I felt down and desperate about my future and what I was going to do. It took almost a year of trying before someone took me on in a job that worked out. It's funny how in life, sometimes someone kind comes along when you really need it, and offers you their hand. Marg, my boss at a home nursing service, was an older, stocky woman who had short wiry hair and a private smile. She didn't say much, but when she spoke, I listened. She mentored me and helped build my confidence. It only took a few simple words of encouragement to give me enough self-assurance to take the next step. About eight months into my job she told me I should apply for a role at head office as a secretary for the managing director. It felt out of reach, but I went for the job and I got it.

The women in my new job were also supportive of me – and in life, that is what matters. Everyone needs a foundation to grow from, a place to try new ways of being in the world. They welcomed me into their team, were patient with me while I learnt new skills, and gave me a sense of belonging.

At the same time, I took a second job waitressing on weekends to pay for an apartment I bought when I was twenty years old. My father taught me to be independent. 'Make sure you buy your own place,' he said. 'That way if your partner beats you, you can leave.' It was odd advice, but sensible. My father was always a pragmatic man. So when my boyfriend of five months put his hands around my throat for getting my hair cut without telling him, I knew what I should do. But I was young and full of self-doubt, and acting decisively was not yet a habit I'd formed. Like many people in relationships with a partner who treats them badly, I found it difficult to leave. I felt torn; there had been many tender moments between us. It was a much smaller moment that ultimately prompted me to end the relationship: he couldn't be bothered turning up to see me on my birthday. We had plans and he just didn't show. That's what made me finally leave – the unbearable feeling that I didn't matter.

Sometimes we know what to do and we live with the shame of doing nothing. Sometimes we find the strength to say that's enough, this relationship no longer serves me well, and we walk away. If that confidence doesn't develop in us, or is lost to us as children, as adults we have to find other ways to build faith in ourselves and learn healthy or sustainable ways to manage the difficult times.

When I was twenty-one, I bought a return air ticket, left my job and with little more than a backpack, a tiny camera and a change of clothes, I took off to roam the world. I didn't know how long I'd be gone – perhaps a few months, or a few years – it didn't matter, I had nowhere to be. My only commitment, my mortgage, was being serviced by the tenants who were then renting my place. I hitchhiked to places that fed my soul and sometimes I cut people's hair very badly for a meal. I found myself growing more confidence and in London, where I landed for a while, I was offered a job as a secretary for a lawyer with a large company.

'Have you got any other clothes?' the recruiter asked. I didn't. 'You'll be working at a corporate office so you'll need a jacket. See if this fits.' It did. I was touched when she offered to give me a few pieces of her own that she no longer needed. My boss, an older, doddery but articulate man, was very friendly, supportive and respectful.

It was a few years later that I returned home, in need of a job and broken-hearted. I'd met a man in London who I found easy to love. But after eight months together, as we lay side by side in bed, he said, 'This is nice, but I don't love you.' When I arrived in Sydney just after midnight I pulled out two scrunched-up twenty dollar notes my father had given me before I left. 'Here's some money for a taxi for when you get back,' he'd said before he gave me a quick awkward hug, and he and Mum had waved goodbye.

By my late twenties I was personal assistant to the group general manager in a large Australian company. But I was treading water: I no longer found secretarial work challenging. I started thinking of other things I might like to do. I was working full-time and volunteering on a crisis line as well as emotionally supporting people who were dying from AIDS, and it was at this point in my life that I thought about working as a counsellor. Born a girl in a traditional migrant family in Bankstown, there was never any talk of going to university or having a career, so it wasn't something I considered previously or thought I could do. Those aspirations were left to the boys. I decided to talk to my boss about studying.

'You're wasted here,' she said. Nothing more. So powerful were those words that my throat constricted and I walked away, my eyes filled with tears. It was a warm feeling to know there was someone who saw my potential. Having someone believe in me gave me the confidence I needed to move forward with a new career. With new determination, I dived back into the deep end to study psychology.

When I sit in my office and wait for clients to arrive, I wonder what will they bring and how I might help. What have they endured to make them who they are and how do they cope with their day-to-day struggles? Do they feel loved, have they had their hearts broken and have they met people who have been kind to them?

We are all complex and our journey is often not straightforward. We don't get everything we wish for. We can't always control what happens to us. Somehow we need to learn to make meaning of what we have and what we create for ourselves. It seems so long ago now, but I remember when my kindergarten teacher asked us what we wanted to be when we grew up. Life was simple then. I wanted to be a giraffe.

These days, I am aware of my mortality and what I haven't had or done in my life. But I'm also more solid than I have ever been. There is a calm in me that allows me to be reflective, to think things through for myself and for others. Through my own experiences I learnt how important the nurturing and support of others can be to instill confidence, develop a sense of self and help someone attain their goals.

I've come to understand that each of us is a work in progress and that it's okay to sometimes fumble through life and learn new ways of being in the world and in relationships. Accepting that we're not perfect is a good thing, being vulnerable is okay, and talking to someone you trust can be helpful.

A fortunate working life – Jenny Smithson

I didn't set out to choose a career over children. But poor choices of partners found me, by the age of thirty, divorced, childless and involved with an older married man who'd already had too many wives and enough children. So my personal life had its limitations, and I turned to my professional life to find satisfaction.

I am a fourth-generation, white, middle-class Australian, the second eldest of five girls all born in the 60s. I wasn't the smartest or the prettiest as a child. I had a 'short back and sides' haircut and wore glasses.

My results suffered in high school when image started to matter. I couldn't see the blackboard sitting with the kids in the back row, and I wouldn't wear my glasses because that wouldn't be cool. I aimed to finish high school and scrape into something at university but had no real idea what; I was more interested in boyfriends and having a good time. It would be fair to say that I was a wild child in my teens.

My father would deny this, and I love him dearly, but when I was in my last year of high school, he asked me what I wanted to do when I finished – perhaps university wasn't for me? That shocked me. It was the first time I realised my parents wouldn't just keep paying for me forever and that I had to prove myself.

So I knuckled down, but study didn't come easily. I

didn't like or couldn't do the hard maths and sciences. I preferred English, history and geography, subjects that gave me limited career options.

Then, in a university careers book, I found a profession called Town Planning. I had never heard of it, but the core subjects were the ones I liked. Better still, I had a high enough entry score to be accepted into the course. The university rang me, I went in for an interview, said I couldn't draw if that was required (it wasn't), and they persuaded me to enrol. And I never looked back.

I have never been afraid to make my own way in life. I met my husband studying planning at university, and we had a long-distance relationship in the early 80s while I worked in a temporary role as a planner for the Albany Town Council and enrolled in a postgraduate degree in his hometown of Sydney.

I moved to Sydney to be with him and completed my master's degree at Sydney University at night, working as a council planner during the day. In those days, walking through Redfern to attend night lectures was an education in itself, and my friends were horrified that I did so on my own, but in the 80s, the night streets of Redfern were alive with activity, and girls from Perth thought it was safe to walk at night alone.

In the late 80s, I convinced my husband to return with me to Perth. The only job either of us could get was the one I was offered by a small multi-disciplinary engineering firm, BSD Consultants, who interviewed me over the phone, offered me a job sight unseen, and paid some of our relocation costs back to WA.

I assumed I would hate working for the private sector and 'greedy developers', but I decided to stay at least six months to repay BSD for giving me a job. I stayed twenty-eight years, grew with the company and became a director, part-owner and, at one point, managed the largest planning consultancy in WA. The first eighteen years were with BSD, the last ten with the company that acquired BSD in 2004.

Being a woman and a planner in a male-dominated engineering firm wasn't easy. Drinks on a Friday night, until I had a say in it, were beer or beer. In the early years, I worked long hours – sixty a week was common – and I thought that working weekends was normal. Other people went home to their families, but I didn't have one: my marriage broke up in the early 90s. My parents thought I was choosing my career over my husband, but that wasn't the case. I just married the wrong person.

From those beginnings, I became many things in my career, often simultaneously. I worked for some amazing clients, met movie stars and sports heroes, the who's who of the Perth social scene of the booming 80s and buoyant 90s, mentored young professionals and toiled alongside colleagues, many of whom became lifelong friends.

In 1996, I was a finalist for the WA Citizen of the Year for my contribution to my profession. I was thirty-three. I had recently been appointed to the board of BSD, and was the most senior female employee in the company.

I was also the WA President of the Planning Institute of Australia. On the morning after the Australia Day long weekend that year, a young admin assistant at BSD, Sarah, was supposed to have finished typing some Institute meeting minutes for me. I recall being annoyed that she hadn't come to work on time to finish those minutes.

Sarah vanished that long weekend. Two other young women subsequently disappeared and their bodies were found. Sarah has never been found.

How my emotions changed over the hours, days and years when I realised she would never come back.

We left her workstation and named coffee cup untouched for as long as we could. Everyone I knew wanted to talk about their theory of what had happened. The night she disappeared, Sarah had been waiting for a cab, but by the time it arrived there was no sign of her. Perth was notorious back then for how long it took to get cabs. These were the days before mobile phones and Uber, and as a young woman I also had waited at night for cabs that didn't come, once walking alone for several kilometres to get home.

I wrote a letter to the newspaper saying that women were being left in vulnerable positions at night and they should drink and drive rather than waiting for cabs that never arrived, because losing their licence was better than losing their life. It was an irresponsible suggestion but it was what I felt at the time.

I had recurring dreams of Sarah being held in a basement of a house, close to the river; I could see a street sign but I couldn't read the name. I drove the streets of Claremont looking for that house. I ended up in police headquarters, at their suggestion. I felt stupid being there but they were amazingly supportive and said they never discounted clues, whatever the medium.

Several months after Sarah's disappearance, I was interviewing a girl for a job and she told me she read my letter to the paper and that I was right. I told her I wasn't, but asked her if what happened to Sarah had changed her. I was heartened to hear that she never walked or waited alone at night anymore.

Last year, as I began writing this, a man was arrested in connection with the disappearance of Sarah and the murder of the two other girls. I hope this leads to closure for their families, and that justice is done.

In the late 90s, I got an opportunity to step outside my traditional planner role, and I was grateful for it. The Shire and Town of Albany councils were to amalgamate to form a new city council. The councillors resigned and the state government appointed commissioners. There was a desire to include women in government appointments, but not many had the professional background and the personal flexibility to take on a part-time, short-term commitment. I had the right skill set and I knew someone who worked for the local government minister. I was appointed to the council as a commissioner, taking unpaid leave and working extra hours at BSD to have time off so I could attend council meetings.

Albany was where I had my first planning position, and where my former husband was now a local planning consultant. He often had matters before council. His new wife was a journalist with the local paper, covering council meetings. We had no conflicts, personally or professionally, although one fellow commissioner commented wryly that there were often too many of us with the same surname at meetings.

Throughout most of my working life, I have been a woman in a man's world. Two particular encounters with men in the course of my career stand out as disappointing examples of the inequality that still exists in the workplace, no matter how competent or accomplished the woman.

In the first encounter, I found myself on a flight seated next to a man with whom I worked but who was also, in terms of the pecking order, my superior. Let's call him 'the statesman'. This man was well-known and twice my age, with daughters older than me. An hour from landing, he put his hand on my thigh and slid it up my skirt. Before it – his hand, not the flight! – could reach its destination, I knocked it away and gripped my hands over my lap. My mind was in turmoil. Even with what I'd experienced in my professional career, where older, usually married, men often surprised me with their unwelcome advances, this was a new low. My shock was followed by sadness, well before any anger arrived. Earlier in the flight he'd offered to drive me home, but when we landed I rushed off to find the cab rank.

It wasn't the first time and it wouldn't be the last that a man used a position of power to try it on. I knew I would have to work closely with the statesman for some time, and I was realistic – who was I compared to this respected elder statesman? Such things, if not commonplace, were not unusual and, after all, what had he really done? Whilst a father or partner might express outrage, in my experience most men would say everything from 'good on him for trying at his age' to 'you should be flattered'. Women would sympathise with me and say 'what a sleaze', and that would be it. This was an appointment I valued – did I want to be seen as a precious, overreacting hysteric the government would regret appointing?

I was on my own; it was my problem to solve. After thinking the matter through, I asked the statesman to have lunch with me. He happily obliged, perhaps assuming I wanted to progress a personal relationship. During lunch I tried my first line of attack, asking him how he would feel if someone of his age did to his daughters what he had done to me. He shrugged and said, 'So, you aren't interested then?'

Moral outrage clearly was not going to work. I changed tack. I said firmly that if he ever touched me again I would go public and I would take action. They were hollow threats really – this man had accolades for his services to the community. But he didn't touch me again.

Although I didn't show it, I was shaking throughout that lunch, while he was totally unaffected. Afterwards I enquired about his reputation from colleagues who'd worked with him. I was told of rumours of women who left quickly, and that he demanded his secretary take dictation on his lap. But no charges were ever laid against him. This is a familiar story, and at that time, it seemed that women had to tolerate and accept it. What alternative did you have? Who could you tell who would do anything about it?

Fast-forward a couple of decades, to a time not so long ago – you might hope that the world had moved on. But my second encounter showed that it has not. I choose to call this man 'the bully', because this time it was not a case of sexual advances but rather of his attitude towards me as a woman, relative to my peers. When I queried why I was offered board tenure renewals of only one year when my male colleagues were offered multiple years, the bully simply withdrew any offer of renewal and I lost my position, despite being praised for my performance by my peers. I knew my initial appointment was not only because of my professional background but because they needed a woman on the team; I believe I am no longer there because I was not sufficiently token or compliant. What disappointed me most of all was that (male) colleagues expressed shock and disappointment at the bully's decision and at other examples of how I had been treated by him, and still did nothing.

I decided, however, that life was too short, and my mental and personal well-being too important for me to pursue any form of discrimination action. I consoled myself with the belief that, with time, the rule and influence of such men – who are of a certain era – will come to an end. My only regret was supporting that same man when a female executive raised bullying allegations against him partway through my term. I should have done more to investigate her claims – he was a bully and he got away with it.

Clearly, as women in the workplace, we have a way to go yet.

I found a more positive response and what I consider to be a more enlightened European attitude in the late 90s when, through BSD, I was tasked by the European Space Agency to help them gain approvals to erect an antenna in WA to track the *Rosetta* spacecraft on its mission. The foothills of Perth were first proposed as the site of the antenna but it wasn't welcomed by the locals, who seemed to believe that it was some sort of covert spy operation.

Working with the Spanish project manager, I instead looked to sites around the wheatbelt town of New Norcia, known for its beautiful stone monastery and Spanish Benedictine monks. After breaking bread together and conversing in their native tongue with the project manager, the monks found the Agency a suitable site for the antenna, and construction began in the early 2000s.

Buried beneath that antenna is a time capsule with the names of those who helped to erect it, including mine. One hundred years from the day it was buried, the capsule will be dug up and I will supposedly be remembered, although doubtfully by anyone who actually knew me.

My life took a more philanthropic turn around that time when, for ten days in 2000, I went to East Timor as one of three volunteers from the Planning Institute of Australia to assist local planning, engineering and architectural students and practitioners to establish a professional institute. I had the support of both the then WA Minister for Planning, whose son had served in East Timor, and the then Shadow Minister for Planning, who had been a UN observer during the independence elections. On her behalf, I took some books to a local missionary.

On arrival, we met with the eager first members of the fledgling institute and began almost immediately to help draft their constitution. We walked through the broken city of Dili and its beautiful countryside devastated by conflict. I slept in a shipping container, rode in tanks with UN soldiers, ate a humble lunch from a communal pot of cabbage in the ruins of the university, and wondered what the future held for the world's newest nation. I helped the institute establish guiding principles to sustainably develop their country. They asked what Australia's guiding sustainability principles were. I still don't know the answer.

Not long after returning, I was appointed as a commissioner for the City of Cockburn. The council there had been dismissed pending a corruption inquiry, and I served two years as deputy chair whilst it played out. As has been my observation of such inquiries, thick reports were produced, people's reputations were sullied, but nobody went to jail.

After serving on Cockburn Council, and whilst still working full-time for BSD, I applied for and was appointed as a part-time member of the newly formed WA State Administrative Tribunal (SAT). This was a big step for my personal accountability. As a council commissioner, I had always made decisions collectively, with the council. Now, for the first time, my individual decisions directly impacted the lives of others.

I remember lunching with a former chairman of the West Coast Eagles and being feted by him to the restaurant owner as one of the most influential women in Perth. Even now, when I look around the city, I can see the physical impact I have had, in buildings, in suburbs, streets and houses. I also think of all the young people who worked for me at BSD and who have gone on to successful careers, many of whom stay in touch.

In 2006, I moved back to Sydney with the global company that acquired BSD, one of fewer than ten female senior principals of over eight thousand staff internationally. This was largely a mentoring role and, with time on my hands, a belief that I could have made quite a good lawyer, and my experience on SAT, I applied for and became a part-time (acting) commissioner of the NSW Land and Environment Court, a role which became permanent in August 2016 when I decided it was finally time to quit consulting and the private sector.

I met my partner in 2013. He has made me appreciate that life holds much more than work, and that every extra hour we work, we dilute the hourly rate we are paid, and therefore our value. He and I have the benefit that neither of us really needs to work and that is the best situation to be in – when you choose to work because you like it, not because you have to.

The same week I was advised that my time on the board in WA wouldn't be extended, he was told his contract role would also be finishing early. We decided to celebrate rather than mourn, and spent nineteen weeks travelling around Europe. Having gained a taste for extended travel, this is now our long-term aim, along with spending more time with our ageing parents and extended families.

Last year, I woke to the news that the *Rosetta* spacecraft had successfully intercepted a comet some eighteen years after I found its tracking antenna a home in New Norcia. At that moment, I understood that sometimes what you do in life makes a difference that is not always evident to you at the time; and that loving what you do, and participating in shared endeavour, can lead to unexpected, if not always tangible, rewards.

Flying kites – Mehreen Faruqi

I don't think I ever had a burning desire to be a politician, but I'm quite sure my relentless questioning about why girls were not allowed to do the same things as boys drove my mother to the end of her tether.

Growing up in Lahore, on the top of my list was doing everything my two older brothers were allowed to do – stay out late at night, play cricket, fly kites on the large cement rooftop of my home, study engineering and work professionally. Permission from my parents to play cricket and fly kites was hard fought, while studying and working as a civil engineer came much more easily.

In my early teens I often sneaked up to the roof, quiet as a mouse, on a rickety bamboo ladder outside our kitchen door, to join my brother and his friends flying kites till I was 'discovered' and hauled down by my mother yelling, 'Mehreen, come down this minute. You know you shouldn't be up there with the boys! You will ruin your complexion!'

Climbing to the roof and my mother's protestations happened almost every day during the spring kite season until my mother finally gave in to what she called my 'stubbornness'. This same persistence served me well in negotiating a truce on cricket. While I wasn't allowed to play with my older brother and his friends, I did get permission to play with the younger brothers of my girlfriends in the neighbourhood, as long as it was in the front yards of our homes and not on the local community cricket pitch. I remember summer evenings spent hitting fours and sixes, the elation felt at making more runs than the boys, and going home to eat luscious, juicy mangoes to celebrate a game well played.

Now, as an MP in the NSW Parliament, those childhood tussles in Pakistan are a distant memory, but my passion to change what I see as unfair has not dampened. The reasoning, skills and determination I honed on my mother come in handy in the political arena, helping me to contest long-held views and archaic laws that need changing, from decriminalising abortion in NSW, to marriage equality and fighting racism.

In a strongly patriarchal society, where there are clearly discriminatory laws and sexist attitudes working against women, I was lucky enough to have a father who valued equal education for his sons and daughters (all four of us did civil engineering as our first degree). For my father, also a civil engineer, a good education was as much about opening up your mind to think deeply and critically as it was about increasing the capacity for earning a good income. Both he and my mother resisted attempts from family members and friends to find me a 'suitable boy' right after I had finished high school.

Knowingly or unknowingly, a number of women have had a profound influence on the choices I've made in life. The four that stand out are my mother, my grandmother, my paternal aunt and my mother-in-law. All of these women taught me, in their unique ways, to be strong and to live life with meaning and purpose. Their guidance, advice and love have given me the resilience and passion to help make me who I am today. I hope to do the same for my daughter.

My mother is generous, kind and trusting. She is the favourite aunt, and the loving niece and daughter of the family. Friends and family turn to her for advice, and more often than not she puts others' needs before her own. These traits could well brand her as a typical 'mother', always ready to sacrifice herself to nurture others. But her very gentle and acquiescing nature hides strength within.

She rode a bicycle to college in the 50s, she travelled the world with my father, leaving their three young children (I was two years old at the time) in the care of her parents, and she embraced social media and email when she was in her sixties. While some of her attitudes are quite conventional, in many other ways she pushes boundaries without making a fuss, and still shows me how to break the mould. I think she learnt this from her mother who was fun, active, dynamic and independent well into her eighties. In my grandmother's home, I was free to play cricket and fly kites to my heart's content, morning, noon or night.

My aunt was a writer, a poet, an activist and feminist. Her husband passed away when I was four and I always saw her as fiercely independent. On extended family gatherings when discussions around the dining table turned to heated debates on politics and religion, she was often the only female voice arguing loudly for women's rights and progressive politics. She was spunky and fiery and her views connected very deeply with me. Given that

I spent a lot of time with her, I'm sure my urge for gender equality is her direct influence. She taught me to stand up for myself no matter the circumstances.

My mother-in-law left a lasting mark even though she was only in my life for a short period of time. Like my aunt, she was widowed when quite young, and was left with four children aged between eight and eighteen. The respect her three sons have for the women in their lives is testament to what a positive role she played. She died in 2001 shortly after being diagnosed with motor neurone disease. I miss her honest, forthright and wise advice. But what I most admired was her calmness, despite facing difficult circumstances throughout life, and especially the way she did what had to be done without seeking any recognition or reward.

In my own case, I can remember hushed conversations between my parents about one marriage proposal or another. Once I overheard my grandfather chiding my mum. 'You're leaving it too late. Once she becomes an engineer, it will be harder to find a good match. She will be more educated than many men, and she'll have stronger opinions about who to marry.'

I'd get anxious because I wanted to finish my degree and work professionally before getting married. I wasn't even sure if I ever wanted to marry.

I would brace myself to refuse when they came to ask my view. But my parents knew me well by then, and knew what I wanted, so those conversations never happened till I was a fully-fledged engineer working in the largest consulting firm in Pakistan.

As it happened, I met my husband, also an engineer, at work. We secretly fell in love, and our wedding was arranged by my beloved aunt and his aunt, both friends.

People are surprised to hear that I never planned to be a politician, that it all happened quite organically or perhaps accidentally. In fact, I've never been one to rigidly plan, but rather when there's a fork in the road I will take the road less travelled. Growing up in Pakistan in the 60s and 70s in an environment where, for girls and young women especially, many key life decisions are made by their parents or family elders, forward planning just didn't make much sense. So for me, life was more about taking up an opportunity when it arose or fighting a battle when it was needed.

My mother and I often talk about life's quirks that take us in such different directions from what we may have planned. She can't believe her daughter, who resolutely refused to go to school in her early school years, has ended up with a couple of higher degrees, a career in engineering, and is a member of parliament in NSW.

I have to admit, there are days when I'm sitting in the chamber of the oldest parliament in Australia, amongst the rough and tumble of NSW politics, and it seems utterly surreal. After all, I am a political 'outsider' in more ways than one. I grew up a world away. I moved to Sydney from Lahore with my husband and one-year-old son when I was twenty-eight, joined the Greens in my late thirties, and was elected to take up my role as an MP in my forties. I didn't come through the so-called political ranks of student unions, party apparatchiks or political staffers, but after spending a couple of very fulfilling decades working as an academic, and in consulting and local government. Engineering is my career; politics, my calling.

It is undeniable that the gender inequality in my country of birth results in the oppression of women through violence, lack of educational opportunities and limited access to equal work. In my experience, this has fed into the generalised view that Pakistani women have little agency. But Pakistan is a country of huge contradictions. For example, Pakistan had its first woman prime minister decades before Australia. I became more aware of this dichotomy after moving here and realising gender equality is also an issue in Australia.

This is quite opposite to what I had imagined – I had naively believed that patriarchy and sexism were issues no longer existing in the 'West'. The Legislative Council of NSW Parliament, where I sit, is a reminder of how much still needs to be done to close the gender gap. There are only nine women members out of forty-two, the lowest percentage of any house of parliament across the country at the moment. This is also a reminder of how perceptions can be so different from reality.

The culture and values I was surrounded by did not look down on women as they aged, nor did women become invisible. Quite contrary to the stereotype of older women as passive and ineffective, or labelled as hags or witches, I remember my mother, grandmother, aunt and mother-in-law at their most influential, vibrant and independent in their fifties and sixties and even later. And beyond them, I was surrounded and loved by doctors, musicians, artists, teachers and scholars, stay-at-home mums, nannies and house help – a big community of women mostly a generation older than me.

The notion of a stereotypical Pakistani woman, or indeed a typical Australian woman, of any age, is alien to me. My life's journey continues to be unconfined by labels. If this were not the case, would I have completed a master's degree and a PhD as a mother with two young children and in my late thirties? Or gone into politics for that matter, at an age when society deems women to be invisible? Perhaps not.

Of course, everyone's life is about give and take, and mine is no different. There have been great opportunities throughout my career, but I would be lying if I said it has all been easy. Moving to Australia and starting from scratch was challenging. I had a husband and a baby son, and dreams of further study. We didn't have jobs or any friends or relatives in Sydney. It took just one flight across the Indian Ocean to leave a whole life behind and with it the web of connections that had supported me till then. During the first few months in Sydney, I was sure we'd made the wrong decision. The isolation and loneliness made a gaping hole that was filled by my tears almost every night.

In Pakistan, society is close-knit and extended families often very large. Mine was no exception. My siblings and I were constantly surrounded by cousins, aunts, uncles, friends and people visiting our home or staying over (sometimes for weeks). This brought both pleasure and pain as we all learnt to share, negotiate and often give in to the needs and wants of others.

Embracing Australia as my home has been both challenging and extraordinarily rewarding. I brought with me my idea of a shared sense of living, and discovered the value Australians place on individuality. It was a constant negotiation between the two worlds and I was drawn to both. Lahore comes alive at night with shopping, eating out and visiting friends and family. When I arrived in Sydney, everything except pubs shut down at five pm. As teetotallers we ruled out the bars. Kings Cross became our Lahore in those early days. Pushing our young son in a stroller, we'd walk up and down Darlington Street, enjoying the lights, sounds and movement. Little did we know that the Cross was perhaps as inappropriate a place for a two-year-old as a pub! Over time, Sydney has changed and so have I. The local drinking hole is now a common venue for many meetings. I never would have thought that one day I would be hosting a public forum on legalising cannabis for adult recreational use in a pub.

Often people ask how I can identify both as an Australian and a Pakistani, but for me it was never a process of making lists of what I liked about either culture and then picking the traits I wanted. It happens as you live life. I don't like vegemite, but am addicted to peanut butter. Does that make me any less Australian? I love the very Australian (and Pakistani) sport of cricket. Where does that put me on the spectrum of belonging?

In a post-9/11 world, people have also questioned my sense of belonging based not on my cultural background but on my faith. Recently, a crude caricature of Muslim women has been created by some in Australia. Being a Muslim woman in the public eye, I am told I am not free, that I am under the control of my husband and that every statement I make on any issue is influenced by my faith or motivated by a hidden agenda to change the so-called Australian way of life. I am told to go back to where I came from.

I've been told that white Australia is the real victim here. I get 'Fuck off, you Muslim turd, and take your halal with you', or 'Don't like it? Well there's plenty of room in the cesspit you and yours crawled out of', and more. I am sometimes not wanted in Australia because I'm a Muslim, which makes me incompatible with the supposedly modern and enlightened Australian way of life. But when I campaign for progressive change that most Australians want and support, such as abortion law reform, voluntary assisted dying, or the legalisation and regulation of adult use of cannabis, then suddenly those same people with their narrow views criticise me for not being a good Muslim. Their claims contest and question my 'Australianness' at every turn. I'm damned if I do and damned if I don't.

For some, migrants of any persuasion will never be truly Australian, a strange contradiction in a country where a vast majority came from somewhere else.

The strong partnership between my husband and I is what has sustained us. Both of us have been able to make a home in a new place and follow a path that is mostly self-determined.

I love my life and try to live it to the fullest. My husband often nags me for not knowing my limits, for pushing myself too hard. These reproaches come after I've been running around and working for days without a break. However, his most recent reprimand came when I complained about aches and pains after playing cricket at the SCG as part of the NSW MPs team against the press gallery and Federal MPs in early 2017.

He was concerned I might get injured since I hadn't played cricket for two decades. But I did play, returning to those days with my friends' brothers in the front yards of our Lahore homes. My husband was there in the spectators stand to cheer me on – the only woman player on either team. It is with his unreserved love, support and encouragement, and the trouble-making streak I was perhaps born with, a streak buffed and polished by the amazing women in my life, that I have been able to boldly take up opportunities that may have been denied to me otherwise. And it is the rejection of these limits that society imposes on women, of what we should or shouldn't do, or who we can or cannot be at a certain age that lets me be who I am, wherever I am.

Djana ngayu – Who am I? – Pat Mamanyjun Torres

Ngayu ngarrangu jarndu. Ngayu Djugun ngany, Jabirr-Jabirr ngany, Nyul-Nyul ngany, Bard ngany, Yawuru ngany, Karajarri ngany. I am Aboriginal woman. I belong to Djugun, Jabirr-Jabirr, Nyul-Nyul, Bard, Yawuru and Karajarri. My Aboriginal name is Mamanyjun, which is a red coastal berry (Mimusops elengi) that grows in the rainforest areas of our clan estates in Jabirr-Jabirr country. I am a strong and proud woman from the First Peoples of Australia. I am connected to Djugun, the original people of the Broome region, Jabirr-Jabirr, the original people of regions north of Broome and west of Beagle Bay. I am also connected to the Nyul-Nyul and Bard, who originated from areas north of Broome, and the Yawuru and Karajarri from areas to the south. I am also Scottish, English, Irish, Filipino and Surabaya-Indonesian on my mother's side. I am approaching *mirdanya*, elder-status, and am in the 'autumn years' of my life. My children are Emmanuelle, Ramiquez, Gabrielle, Karim and Tornina. I currently have five grandchildren, Joriah, Evander, Kazali, Jivan and Angelous, all boys.

My mother is Mary Theresa 'Warrarr' Barker, descended from apical ancestors Milare and Keleregodo, who gave birth to Ida Mathilde Tiolbodonger, who married Catalino

Torres, a Spanish-Filipino, and gave birth to Joseph Torres, my mother's father. My mother's mother Irene Drummond is a descendant of Mary Minyirr aka Mary Minyarl (Djugun) and Mary Bajinka II (Yawuru-Karajarri).

My father, John McGregor, is an Australian-born Scotsman descended from Hughie McGregor who came from Glasgow, Scotland, and Stella Cook from Dandaragan, near Perth, Western Australia. The continuing effect of the colonisation of Australia has meant that I have had minimal contact with this side of my family despite my attempts to be connected. Perhaps this is one reason why I am so passionate about my Aboriginal family lines, their histories and our knowledge systems.

My life has been an extraordinary one, full of stories of our families' social and cultural histories, and how we interconnect with Australia's First Peoples in the Kimberley region, and the Asian and European immigrants who came to live and work in this part of Australia. Many diverse peoples married our womenfolk from the Djugun, Yawuru, Jabirr-Jabirr and other people, thereby creating my descent line of the Torres and Drummond families. I have grown up with a great thirst and hunger for knowledge and am privileged to live in a time when Australian society is more supportive of Australia's First Peoples, in comparison to the previous generations of my mother, grandmother and great-great-grandmother.

My great-great-grandmother, known as Mary Minyarl, was a Djugun woman from Ngunu-ngurra-gun, now known as Coconut Well, situated north of Broome, Western Australia. She lived at a time when women were kidnapped off the coast, enslaved in chains and forced to free dive for pearl shell for the early master pearlers. Mary Minyarl was removed from her family clan lands in Djugun country, and taken north into Jabirr-Jabirr clan lands to dive for pearl shells. She was also taken south into Yawuru lands along the coast to collect the large pearl shells with other Aboriginal women. These pearl shells created wealth and influence for early colonial families in Western Australia.

Eventually, in a southern Asian camp located in Yawuru country, Mary Minyarl met her husband, Abdul bin Drummond from Surabaya. Their son, Karim Drummond, was born on Yawuru country near Yadjugan. Great-Grandfather Karim, known as Injalman, was my grandmother Irene's father. Karim had a sister, Mercedes Drummond, who we called Great-Granny Matjis. When my great-grandfather Karim grew up, he had to learn how to live with three laws: Aboriginal, Muslim and White Australian. He learnt about Aboriginal law from his mother's relations and Aboriginal uncles. He learnt about Muslim law from his father's side, and he learnt about Australian law after marrying my great-grandmother Mary Theresa 'Polly' Fitzpatrick and getting locked up for cohabitating with an Aboriginal person.

The funny thing about the last one is that my great-grandfather Karim was also a 'native', but the authorities chose to label him as an Asian, and in those days Asians were prohibited from fraternising with Aboriginal people. But my great-grandfather was indeed an Aboriginal person. I remember seeing on his chest the initiation scars called *mugadal* when he was performing a healing ritual after I contracted tetanus as an infant. He had a pierced nasal septum and pierced earlobes for the placing of carved items, which marked his status as a man of 'high degree' in Aboriginal law. He was also a *maban* man, a spiritual healer who gave me the gift of a yellow-and-white-feathered emu chick as a spirit-being, that grew into a spiritual protector keeping me from harm. I remember seeing the small golden-white feathers cupped in his hands and hearing the chirping sound of the chick. I was only two years old at the time.

My experiences with, and inheritance of, Aboriginal spiritual knowledge, and extensive spiritual events throughout my life have given me a strong belief in the power of our ancient knowledge and belief systems. It has provided me personally with many sustaining ideals of family, identity and culture, which has provided me with a passion and a purpose to protect and maintain our cultural practices and linguistic knowledge about plants, people and our environment.

Before British invasion and colonisation of Australia there existed more than 750 languages and dialects, and just as many cultures, in this land we now all call home. My Djugun, Jabirr-Jabirr, Nyul-Nyul, Bard, Yawuru and Karajarri ancestors from the West Kimberley region of Western Australia saw the world through concepts called *bugarrigarra* (dreaming histories) and *yamminga* (ancestral times), both concepts that explain the early history of people, place and language. These concepts embody stories of the creative activities of ancestral beings, where the land is sacred, and the animals, plants, people and environments are closely interconnected. These ancestral creation stories are still held sacred today.

My identity and experiences have also been formed through the colonising experience, where labels of Aboriginality and authenticity have been constructed by others, often to the detriment of the First Peoples and their communities. For us, this colonising experience has been long, damaging, and brutal. We continue to experience this brutality on many levels in twenty-first century Australia. More than twenty years have passed since the Native Title Act of 1993, where Aboriginal common law rights were compromised to include the right to be consulted only. Even more years have passed since the 1400s when the first waves of invasion began with the privateers under the banner of 'discovery and empires' for the kings and queens of their European countries. The mass invasion of the 1770s by the British colonial forces under the myth of 'terra nullius' and its treatment of Australia's First Peoples has created a mindset that continues up to the present. In this contested space, we strive to analyse the meanings behind colonial words like 'aborigine', 'indigenous', 'settler', and 'settlement', to name a few.

The complicated layers of colonial history and its impact on First Australians is slowly being acknowledged by wider society, where many are genuinely interested in rectifying past wrongs. We are all connected to this history. Its continuing effects on future harmonious and peaceful interrelationships within our diverse nation are not just an Aboriginal problem, but an issue for all Australians to face head-on. Together we must make informed decisions about how we are going to respond as twenty-first century Australians to continuing injustices against First Peoples.

My personal journey has been driven by a commitment to improve the lives of Australia's First Peoples, as I have experienced firsthand the inequalities that exist. My experiences have been intrinsically shaped by being a woman descended from Australia's First Peoples. I am a person of colour, of mixed heritage, possessing a strong identity informed by Australia's First Peoples' traditions and worldviews, despite my pale-coloured skin.

My thirst for ancient knowledge has led me along a journey towards *nilangany*, that is, to be 'possessed by knowledge', seeking the spiritual and epistemological pathways to acquire understanding of my ancient peoples and their ways of seeing the world around us. My mother and my brother also felt this need to reconnect with our traditions: my mother participated in traditional women's law during her life, and my brother became an initiated man. He was the first person in our immediate family since my grandmother's brother *mimi* Cassmond Drummond went through men's law during the 1930s, following in the footsteps of my great-grandfather *jalbi* Karim Drummond in the early 1900s. These continuing connections have meant that my family has lived within and between two worlds – the Western and the Indigenous – and we have benefited from the richness of both.

As for me, I was privileged to learn from many family members and extended kinfolk, who were informed by First Peoples' knowledge. This knowledge profoundly affected how I proceeded in my tertiary education choices, and my career in Aboriginal education.

Knowing both Kimberley Aboriginal Australian culture and white Australian culture has meant that my family and I often take on roles that bridge the gap between the two groups. My past careers as a curriculum development officer for the Tasmanian Education Department in Hobart, and with the federal Department of Education and Youth Affairs in Broome, Darwin and Canberra, are examples of this bridging role.

Our families, who live at the intersection of so many different identities, have been at the forefront of language, health, education, music, arts and cultural programs. We do this to achieve positive life changes for our extended families and remote communities, as well as to facilitate cross-cultural understandings in the mainstream Australian contexts. I believe that knowledge provides understandings and the power to make informed decisions so you can have a more enriched and satisfying life where you can thrive and not just survive.

Change is slow, and the achievement for Aboriginal people's rights takes time against the tide of continuing colonisation and its embedded racism and politics of difference. I stand as both witness to, and a participant in, positive actions towards change. Through the commitment of Aboriginal Land Councils, like the Kimberley Land Council (where I worked in the early 1980s) and their workers, some justice and economic benefit for Aboriginal people has been achieved under Native Title determinations. Recently, government agencies have been working out ways to 'Close the Gap' through movements like the 'Recognise' campaign. Today we are experiencing the political issue of First Peoples' sovereignty versus recognition. Through legislation, the federal government is seeking to incorporate Aboriginal and Torres Strait Islander peoples into the Australian Constitution. Much debate surrounds this recent development.

Will this raised consciousness and action create any long-term justice and economic and political change for First Peoples of Australia? We shall see. I remember during the 1980s, when I was a member of the National Aboriginal Education Committee that advised Senator Susan Ryan, we had called for a *makarrata*, or treaty. Now, more than thirty years later, we are still calling for a treaty to negotiate our rights as First Peoples. It takes the concerted efforts of many across time to achieve the final outcomes of equality, fairness and justice for all. And I am one of the many.

On reflecting about my life's journey, I have come to believe that for Australians to truly move forward in social justice, reconciliation and recognition we need a Truth Commission to be established that lays bare the raw truth about Australia's past treatment of its First Peoples – one that can establish both mechanisms and a change of attitude to redress the devastating effects of displacement and exclusion of First Peoples. Only then will we all benefit as twenty-first century Australians, and only then will the First Peoples experience basic human rights taken for granted by so many others. One of my last wishes for my five children and five grandsons is that they will live in a future Australia where they can enjoy the benefits of being an Australian, free from racism, harassment and brutality, and truly experience what other Australians call, 'A Fair Go'.

My mixed heritage identity has made me both a survivor and a thriver. I have loved passionately, lived purposefully and have strived to be respectful and generous towards all peoples. I have valued and cherished my friends and families who have valued me, choosing to retreat to my safe spaces when I have faced too much negativity from those around me. As I have grown older and expanded my interests, knowledge and skills, I have achieved many successes through my fabric artworks featuring traditional symbols, the publication of children books and illustrations, academic pursuits and recently the development of an Australian cuisine through bush tucker and native-plant remedies. I am personally driven by my families' values and our sustaining ideals of land, culture, identity and respect for our language, our knowledge and our *ngarrangu nilangany*, our Aboriginal knowledge and worldview. This knowledge, its concepts and people's relationships between themselves, animals, plants and environments form the *ngarrangu nilangany*, creating what the anthropologist Deborah Bird Rose has called a 'sacred geography' within a 'nourishing terrain'. My life experiences have shown me that it is vital that Australia's First Peoples' voices are heard – to educate Australians about living sustainably within threatened environments, and also to ensure justice and fairness is achieved in Australian society in all its diversity.

Notes

[1] D.B. Rose, 'Sacred geography', *Nourishing Terrains: Australian Aboriginal views of landscape and wilderness*. Canberra: Australian Heritage Commission, 1996.

Seeking singular single older women – Susan Laura Sullivan

I am still sometimes asked if I'm married. It's a question asked and answered with some trepidation. As I age, it's taken for granted that I am or have been, and queries abate. Questions about my supposed husband or partner occur on occasion. Setting people right about not having a partner can be uncomfortable. The stigma of being female, older and unmarried colours the interchange, even if I'm not so worried about the situation. There's no easy fix to breaking the conventions of polite conversation.

I live in Japan. When I arrived in the early 90s, I thought I'd returned to 1950s Australia. My opinion of that era was informed by my mother's words and my perception of the time. Taxi drivers often asked my age and my marital status. Japanese is a hierarchical language and certain phrases are used with particular ages and social positions. The answers to these questions could be used to determine the level of politeness needed to address me.

'Twenty-three,' I'd tell them. 'Not married.'

'*Mada wakai*,' was the response. 'You're still young.'

By the age of twenty-five, though, my youth was null and void. I can't recall the reaction taxi drivers had to my nuptial status; they probably changed the subject. A lot is different now, but in the 90s in Japan, the concept of 'Christmas Cake' was something women under thirty were well aware of. Christmas Eve is an important day for singles taking a potential loved one on a date. Christmas Cake – a fruit, cream and sponge concoction – is part of the equation. The cake stales quickly and can't be sold for optimum value beyond December twenty-five. Women not married by twenty-five were deemed day-old Christmas Cake, 'left on the shelf'. A Japanese businessman I taught in the 90s said he paid his female staff less because he expected them to resign once they reached their mid-twenties.

Australia's public service had similar official policies until 1966.[1] In the 1950s, my mother joined the Kalamunda telephone exchange at age fifteen. By twenty-one, she was a supervisor in Geraldton. After thirteen years of service, she left her job as required by the policies of the time when she married. A woman's choices were limited by her married state, and the married state was the standard at the time. If women had to resign after they wed, and were expected to stay home and raise kids, then this was their public face – not public at all.

The Christmas Cake notion is no longer as prevalent in Japan, though many pregnant women still leave work due to company and cultural pressure. The average age for marriage among the population now is approximately thirty for women, and thirty-one for men.[2] One in seven Japanese women are still single by the time they are fifty, not including those divorced and widowed.[3] De facto relationships, in the Australian sense, aren't common. Being independent can be explored, but often at the expense of relationships or kids.

Among the Japanese and Western women I know here, some have deliberately chosen careers over having children. Others chose not to have relationships and, in a conservative society like Japan, that generally entails no kids. It's commonly accepted that relationships lead to marriage, and children follow. Child rearing is mostly undertaken by women.

Single women who *are* seeking relationships are often expected to put in so much time at work, in part due to perceived lack of family commitments, that their chances of meeting someone narrow significantly. Women go against the grain by choosing a career, and for many women it also means remaining single.

Wherever I have lived, positive role models for those of us not married have been hard to come by, particularly as I've aged. If you fall outside of the coupled norms, it's best to keep your own counsel to maintain confidence. Betsy Israel's work, *Bachelor Girl: The Secret History of Single Women in the Twentieth Century*, outlines US government and media attitudes of the late 1800s, critical of women who didn't end up in heteronormative relationships, including choosing to be single. The media maintained this attitude throughout the next century, using scare tactics such as painting a lonely and bitter old age for the single woman.[4]

As I was growing up, I thought there were only two relationship statuses: married and not married. My great-aunt Mag moved in with my grandparents and uncle in their Perth home after the last of her goldfields siblings had passed away. Never married, she was the stereotypical doting spinster aunt in my mother's childhood and my own. Despite this, I viewed Mag's dependence as weak.

Her brother-in-law, my grandfather, seemed to regard her with annoyance.

I felt pity for her, in the way a ten-year-old trying to be whatever normal is. I knew little of Mag's achievements, which included teaching, helping migrants on the goldfields with English, supporting the ALP, and looking after my mother's extended and immediate family. My grandmother, on the other hand, never worked outside the home, first having to look after her sick mother, and then taking care of her own children once she married. But that was a sign of the times. Mum always felt if more options had been available for women in terms of schooling, working, and raising families, Nan would have taken them.

I was told the reason for Mag remaining single was that she fell for a Protestant boy. Religious intolerance within our Catholic family prevented her from marrying him. I understood this to mean that not being with someone – either through tragedy or preference – meant you were lacking something. I never entertained an alternative view. Mag, however, may have thought there were advantages to being independent at a time when being married meant losing your job and bearing children. The fact that dying in childbirth was not uncommon might have been deterrent enough.

Mag was born near the turn of the century. Betsy Israel writes that in the US from 1870 to 1914, the marriage rate among women with an education drastically decreased as life paths beyond being a wife and mother opened up.[5] Some of these opportunities no doubt existed in Australia, even though Constance Stone, the first female doctor registered in this country, was barred as a woman from learning medicine at the University of Melbourne, and had to gain her qualifications in North America in the 1880s.[6]

I have had advantages in terms of career and women's rights that my female ancestors did not. I can work *and* enter serious relationships, but in my thirties it seemed unlikely I was going to. I hadn't had much luck with meeting someone to that point and, as such, I actively sought older single role models. There had to be more to life without a partner than loneliness and dependence, or being defined by my relation to another. Mag was a possible role model, but I'd only met her as an elderly woman, and my impressions were shaped by the stories of my grandmother and mother.

Finding successful older female singles wasn't easy. The internet wasn't as streamlined as it is now. Relevant search terms led me to online dating sites, the opposite of what I needed. Many friends spoke of keeping someone in reserve to marry – by mutual agreement – if they hadn't found a partner by thirty. They were joking, but the pressure to *not* be alone was real.

Australia, New Zealand, the US and Japan are relatively accepting places for a single woman to live. I've resided in them all. But the pressure to marry is fairly universal, and the pressure to be with someone is also perhaps biological. There is nothing wrong with being single, but social conditioning is a tough thing to recognise and face, both internally and externally.

An adult Korean student of mine in New Zealand spoke of her family, and how they made her feel she had failed by being single. I told her, more bravely than I felt, that we needed to be our own role models if we couldn't find them in the public domain or in the words of strangers, acquaintances or relatives. Korean children look forward to gifts of money every New Year. An unmarried woman is considered a child and my student still received cash from her relations on January first. She could have exploited the situation, but mostly felt embarrassed. She wrote to me when she returned home to say she'd found someone, and I was happy for her.

Omani attitudes were not that far removed from Korean. I went to the Sultanate in my late thirties, the age my mother had her fourth and last child. When taxi drivers asked if I was married, I'd say I was, and they immediately showed me photos of their family. I wore my grandmother's wedding ring. If I said I was single, suddenly I was fair game. Being without a male companion in a society steeped in machismo, I attracted attention. My behaviour was outside the norm. As such, I was a viable target. Harassment was justifiable even if it was considered haram, not in keeping with Islamic tenets.

When I visited the UAE, a Filipina taxi driver with a degree in business drove me to the airport. She had been hired to drive female customers. She had adult children back home and said there was still time for me to have kids, but I should hurry, given my age. She was a lovely woman and meant well, but I understood that my life choices so far were lacking in her eyes, as well as in the eyes of many other taxi drivers, those bellwethers of a nation.

An Iraqi professor I worked with invited me to her home. Houses in Oman were cheap in terms of my Western concepts and salary. It was a massive place on the beachfront, built to include a few families, the floors made of tile and marble. Sand from the seashore and surrounding desert crept into and over all surfaces. As a divorced woman in Oman, the professor had limited social outlets, and her own role models would have been scarce.

Being married was like turning the pages of the same book, she told me – no longer interesting. She had initiated the separation. At work, I heard constant judgement against her from the male professors who were fluent in English. They sat, scratched and bickered like old chooks. The female professors were just as critical, but there were fewer of them.

Oman opened up in the 1970s. At the time it had only three primary schools, so catching up in terms of education was crucial to the development of the nation. Some of my students' mothers couldn't read. Many women signed their names with an X. I worked with a smattering of Omani instructors, but the majority were from the surrounding countries. Not all were male, but most were.

I taught English to another female professor. She was from Syria. Druze, the other instructors whispered with the kind of aversion the Catholics of my great-aunt's youth held for Protestants. Her husband was studying in Spain.

In a society with very few safety nets for women on their own, these two Iraqi and Syrian professors were basically single mothers, though one had a Filipina live-in maid. The male professors came to Oman with their families, or alone. Some had a family in either place. Marriage and career with support, or without the day-to-day responsibilities of childcare, was an option for the men. Not so for these two women whose situations were mostly viewed as unsound, even while the establishment employed them for their needed skills in mathematics and science.

I admired them. Their English was better than that of many of my international students in New Zealand or Australia, yet their chances of gaining visas to better their lives elsewhere were restricted. In a place where the opportunities to meet someone were slim, and the pressure to be with someone was strong, I can imagine they'd fought to own their identities much longer and harder than I had. To even walk on the beach with someone of the opposite sex who was not family resulted in a chorus of speculation. When some interest was shown between one of these professors and another teacher, the consensus was that she *should* be with someone, but it was still ridiculous that she was seeking someone to be with, especially at her age – and the actions of both instructors were *haram* anyway. Things just weren't done that way.

Before I went to Oman, I learnt the expression *Masha'Allah*: it is God's will. It was a good response to people asking why I wasn't with someone. Or so I thought. Students, teachers and the man or woman on the street all asked why I wasn't married and didn't have kids. Kids often seemed more important than being wed. God's will didn't cut it. There was still time. I should. I could. People prayed my health and well-being would grant me progeny.

Paradoxically, while I tried to find ways to be successfully single, a few relationships crept up on me. I hadn't gone looking for them. This was the first decade of the millennium and I lost a number of years due to them. In fact, I'd gone to New Zealand to start afresh from a failed relationship. From 2012 onwards, I re-emerged unattached and slowly regained the self-knowledge and confidence I find I lose when I am with someone. I grew more content with being alone.

Unlike my mother and many women before her, I freely gave up a lucrative job and the chance of tenure during those unfocused years. I also lost a contract. The appeal of being with someone trumped common sense and making my own way. At one stage, I was in the dangerous position of not having a guaranteed income when I moved to the US for a man. The choice to do so was my own.

My partner was generous, though elements of the relationship were manipulative. Business ventures we'd discussed before I went over didn't eventuate, and my visa didn't allow me to work. If the relationship had been stable, employment opportunities might have arisen once visa issues were sorted. But it never was, and they never were.

It was disconcerting to lose that control over my life. I was in my early forties and I'd rarely relied on anyone else for my day-to-day survival. Capital entails independence. My American partner was well-off and had retired early, in part because of his own efforts, but mostly due to the achievements of his ex-wife. I extracted myself from a vulnerable situation, and returned to Japan.

He visited me, and we shared expenses as we travelled. I was relieved to contribute financially again, even if it wasn't on an equal footing. I'd never make nor save what he and his ex-wife had. Long-distance relationships rarely last the distance though, and we were no exception.

I still live in Japan, and work alongside three other single women, and two married men. One woman is in her late thirties, and the others are in their forties. I'm fast approaching fifty. One professor gained her PhD in the States. The pay-off for doing what she loves was to look after her mother – much as my grandmother did – on her return to Japan. She doesn't seem to resent this. Her brothers are married with kids.

There are many things I might not have seen if I were permanently with someone: the Southern Alps, Okinawan seas, camels sauntering along desert roads. By the same token, there are places I haven't visited, and times I didn't go out, due to lack of companionship. A significant other doesn't guarantee company, though. My American ex liked to sleep late and wasn't keen on hiking, or meandering from one place to the next. Setting my timetable to another's meant seeing a fraction of what I wanted, or striking out as if I were single and reconciling myself to crossing paths with him a few hours a day. Maybe that is what relationships are, but it wasn't enough for me.

That women or men are defined by their attachment to one another has elements of truth and practice within it, but also excludes those who walk different paths. I have traversed a single life with a few deviations, and if I am to be discontent, I'd prefer it to be on my own terms. That is, I'm perfectly happy to be unhappy on my own. The same goes for boredom. Being single is not so bad in a world *where I can earn*, and therefore survive, despite the tremendous push, some of it biological, a whole lot of it psychological, to be with someone.

The pressure for women to comply with societal norms can result in a lifelong lack of upward mobility, as seen in the rising number of older women in positions of poverty, despite, or maybe even because of, years of marriage. In friends and acquaintances, I see a multitude of ways to be normal. Being accepted as such, both inwardly and outwardly is ideal. The trick lies in navigating the terrain.

Notes

[1] Marian Sawer, 'The Long, Slow Demise of the "Marriage Bar"', *Inside Story*, 2016; www.insidestory.org.au/the-long-slow-demise-of-the-marriage-bar/

[2] 'Chapter 2: Population', *Statistical Handbook of Japan 2016*. Tokyo: Japanese Ministry of Internal Affairs and Communication: Statistics Bureau, 2016, p.18; www.stat.go.jp/english/data/handbook/pdf/2016all.pdf

[3] Kyodo, '1 in 4 men, 1 in 7 Women in Japan Still Unmarried at Age 50: Report', *The Japan Times*, 2017; www.japantimes.co.jp/news/2017/04/05/national/1-4-japanese-men-still-unmarried-age-50-report/

[4] Betsy Israel, *Bachelor Girl: The Secret History of Single Women in the Twentieth Century*. New York: Harper Collins, 2002.

[5] ibid., p.30.

[6] Penny Russell, 'Stone, Emma Constance (1856–1902)', *Australian Dictionary of Biography*. Canberra: National Centre of Biography, ANU, 2017; http://adb.anu.edu.au/biography/stone-emma-constance-8676

Living at Clarkie's Camp – Sarah Drummond

Last night I dreamed of the sea eagle. It looked down at me from the spar of a power pole on the overpass into the city. In the morning when I awoke at the inlet it was from the marri tree at the water's edge that the eagle regarded me. It looked sanguine, interested as I called in its own eerie language. Later I saw the bird cruising the shoreline, hunting, wings tilted up like a dancer's fingers, as it does every day. I called again but the eagle ignored me.

When my youngest child left home, I left the city for a place of gothic, dripping cathedrals of trees. It was winter and the potholed and corrugated track to the inlet was littered with curling strips of fallen karri bark and branches. I rented an off-grid cottage at the end of the track crouched under huge marri trees, knotted limbs crazy dancing against a steel grey sky.

Broke Inlet lies thirty-five kilometres from the tiny farming and national parks town of Walpole on the south coast of Western Australia. If you walked through the bracken and zamia palms from my cottage, past the Creepy Shack with its kicked-in asbestos walls, soaked mattresses and magazines from the 1980s, past the massive burled marri that I call my gateway guardian, you will find the townsite of Camfield. Except that this is not a town but a row of jury-rigged shacks. Corrugated iron, salt-faded weatherboards and face cuts gleaned from nearby timber towns, barred windows and padlocks on anything that can be opened or stolen, rainwater tanks, drop dunnies part way up the primary dune to give run to the septic tank or a decent view. The shacks face out to the inlet in a stoic line. Across the water, a break in the coast hills signifies The Cut, where the sandbar breaches once the inlet has swelled to splitting.

I came here to research the story of Clarke, a man consigned to an unofficial witness protection program in the 1920s. Apparently, he lived at a place called Clarkie's Camp, on the same property as me. There must be many other secrets out here but my interest was the secret of Clarke: to divine his presence, to listen for him in the deep, heavy silences of the inlet, when the wind drops and even the birds are censured by lack of sound. An oyster pale Sunday. The crack of my axe, splitting the air.

A kind of folk mythology surrounds Clarke's presence at Broke Inlet.

'Didn't someone live out his days at Broke on the run from the cops?'

'Dad reckoned he was a spy and the government hid him there.'

'Wasn't Clarke that butcher? With the big knife?'

The most common story is that Clarke was stashed at Broke Inlet by the state government, and that, once a month, a policeman would leave him supplies at the turn-off from the main road.

I was in bed and ready for sleep the night my lover's headlights loomed on the bedroom wall, and his big old diesel coughed to a halt. The dog stirred and wagged her tail, friendsome. The glass door slid open and I saw the blue LED glare of his headlamp.

'Hello.'

'Hello,' he said. He paused at the bookshelf, then rushed to kneel at my bedside. 'I have two questions for you … will you marry me?'

And when I said it was a complicated question that required discussion, he said, 'I've got two bottles of red and some dex and I haven't eaten all day and I'd like to spend the night driving around the back roads of Broke with you and do some discussing. What say you?'

It is said women can become invisible at a certain age. But the mistress, that unspeakable woman of any age, is kept hidden inside a walled garden. Some would say it is a purer love, without the contracts and obligations of a marriage. Still, she who resides in her lover's heart remains there on the condition of invisibility, anonymity, and of maintaining the secret. I receive the comment 'I can't believe no-one has snapped you up yet, Sarah' from slightly wistful old men and girlfriends. I say 'comment' rather than 'compliment' because underneath their words I hear the query: 'What is wrong with you?'

I can't tell you the truth about the man who loves me, I'd think.

Truth, in this situation, would create social and marital carnage in our little community of friends. The centre would not hold. I maintained the silence, as so many invisible women have done before me. It was feeling shackled by secrets that also led me to the inlet, where I could yell them out loud, or at least find peace of mind to write through them. By then, our affair had been going on for years.

There was another secret. An old friend, one of the wistful ones, told me something in confidence and this would lead to his suicide two weeks later. During the two weeks, I kept his crimes to myself as he had asked me to but, unbeknownst to me, he was packing up his legacy. He sent his valuables to his son in a trunk, redirected his mail and organised his will. He came to see me two days before he was due to face court. He asked me to call the police at a certain time. He said he didn't want an innocent to find him. I agreed. On my table he placed his will, enough cash to clean out his flat, a ripe avocado and two dozen eggs.

Not long after that I moved out to Broke. Friends say that I changed the day I drove his car away from the towing company and now I think they were right. I had to break the coroner's tape that stuck the car doors shut and the van reeked of exhaust fumes and no-one could ever be the same after a drive like that. Like Tennyson's Lady of Shalott, I was half sick of other people's secrets and foibles. The geographical leap did not keep my lover from me though. He just drove further into the night to find me, bringing me gifts of chainsaws, books, gemstones or rabbit traps.

I found work at a coffee shop in town. Recently, I made drinks for two elderly, lifelong Walpole residents. Two chai lattes. Pat has hers half-strength and wonders if we have any lactose-free milk. Patti's hands are cracked, stained deep with her garden's dirt. They'd just found out I live at Broke Inlet.

'Don't you get scared?' asked Patti.

Perhaps my move to the inlet was a bit reckless. I hauled all of my belongings out here on a car trailer. My final act of commitment was to throw my mattress on the back of the ute. I was moving two hundred kilometres from my home and into the wilderness. The dirt track from the highway was ten kilometres long and flooded on the flatlands where the grass trees and tiger snakes thrived. What was I thinking? No electricity. No internet. No mobile phone range. A dog. No money. This is mad, I thought as the ute thudded along through islands of karri and burnt-out swamps.

I assembled my bed in the lounge room that night, lit the fire and took two benzos; leftover morsels from the panic attacks I experienced after my friend died. I sat up in bed and stared through the big windows into the gloom scrawled with the ancient silhouettes of trees. The moon glowed the water. There was no-one else here but me.

Except there was. My dog burst into hysterical barking at three in the morning. Someone or something was walking around the cottage. I could hear grunts and twigs breaking. Wild pigs? No, because a light flashed. A headlamp perhaps. A gloamy shape walked past the lounge room window. Oh, here we go, I thought.

I was still awake at dawn when my dog barked again. More growling. Two dogs the size of lions sniffed at the door. The neapolitan mastiff's coat was blue, like a burmese cat, his huge head grizzled with folds of skin, a flashing LED light the shape of a bone hanging from his collar. He and the brindle great dane turned and loped away, balls the size of a man's fist swinging against their scarred haunches.

The next day, driving into town for supplies, I met some pig hunters. The first ute full of men stopped beside me on the track and the driver wound down his window. Skinheaded with a scar down the side of his face and another across his forehead, he chewed as he talked, fast. He looked a bit pinned. His voice was gravelly.

'Gidday, love, seen any pigs?'

Once I'd wound down the window, my dog peered over my shoulder and all hell broke loose. On the tray of his four-wheel drive, four lean, whiskery lurchers in leather chest harnesses and bristling GPS wires raised a racket at the sight of my dog. Behind the lurchers was the cage of killers: chunky brindled pig dogs with spike collars and teeth like T-rexes.

'No,' I said in a small voice.

'Well. Whaddya up to then, love?'

'Oh, you know, just heading into town.'

The second ute stopped behind him. Four men and more dogs of the same ilk.

'She's a nice-looking dog you got there. Got a bit of rotti in her, ay? She'd be good to have around. We're going up the Shannon after pigs. Or maybe marron. Seen any marron?'

The dogs were still bellowing, egged on by the ute-load behind them.

'Shut the *fuck* up!'

They drove on, and I drove into town, laughing. The last time I saw men like that was in the Northern Territory.

I thought they were extinct on this gentrified south coast. Straight out of *Mad Max* and here they were on the Broke track. On my return, with shopping bags full of horseradish, cheese, toilet paper, milk, wine and a cooked chook, my internal *Deliverance* scenarios began to do me in. It was pouring with heavy rain, beginning to feel like it would be inches. What if the hunters decided against the Shannon River, sheltered at the huts and started partying? What if they were at my place?

I put my big fishing boots outside the front door to make it look like a man lived there. I walked the hundred metres to the gate and shackled it shut.

'Yeah, I get scared sometimes,' I said to Patti. She stared at me.

'Does anyone else live out there?'

'No.' Lots of people ask me this. 'People come out on holidays and weekends though.'

'A bloke lived at Broke,' Patti said. 'Now. What was his name? My husband took food and supplies out to him. What was his name?'

'Clarke?' I hardly dared to hope. It would have been more than fifty years ago.

'Yes! Clarke. Clarkie. My husband, bless him, he used to do the milk run to Manji once a week. Picked up all the milk and cream along the way. He'd come back from town with everything we needed in Walpole, the kids' shoes, clothes. Took him ten hours or more, that run.'

'He was our lifeline,' Pat nodded, 'in those days.'

'He never told me about that, you know,' Patti said. 'Just before he died, he told me he'd taken food out to that bloke at Broke for decades. Never said a word.'

So that was how Clarke was sustained and remained a secret: the milkman bound to confidentiality by an arm of the law. I wondered about the policeman who was supposed to have dropped supplies for him. There must have been a quarrel in the mind of that copper – feeding the man who'd helped hide the hacked-up bodies of his two colleagues.

In 1926, Clarke testified that he was in the parlour of a Kalgoorlie pub with two of his mates, Coulter and Treffene. He told the court that Coulter had requested Clarke's help. While stealing gold at a plant that morning, they were surprised by the gold squad detectives, Pitman and Walsh. To avoid arrest, Treffene and Coulter shot both detectives in the face. They told Clarke that seeing as he was part of their operation and had a car, he should help them dispose of the bodies. Clarke drove them back to the plant where they cut up the bodies with butcher knives from the hotel kitchen. After a failed attempt at a cremation, Clarke drove through the night, with the hessian-wrapped remains of the policemen in the boot of his car, to an isolated mineshaft.

'Probably best ease up on the mullet stories now,' my lover said one evening. The last time I'd been in town and online, I posted a story on my blog about netting mullet but the net season had officially ended and he is a more cautious soul than me. He has to be.

'A good idea,' I agreed. 'Now, here is a better caution. Could you please take your matrimonial pillow with you when you go home to your family?' I threw the patterned pillow aside. 'It's too weird.'

But he never did. Some balmy summer mornings when he slept in, I'd come out of the shower to see him in my bed, his arms and one knee draped over her pillow and his shaggy head resting on mine.

The dog waited for me ashore, as I rowed out the boat. I thought he was coming to visit me. I'm never sure when he will visit me. Part of being kept secret is the instability and lack of accountability. But he'd said he'd come out this night. If he couldn't make it, I'm out of contact anyway.

I set a mullet net, and stumped up the hill in my fishing boots to make a desultory dinner. When it was past ten o'clock and he still wasn't here, I rowed back out into the inlet. I rowed and rowed and I couldn't find the net. The depleted headlamp had no reach for a little styrofoam buoy. I clicked off the light and waited for my night vision, for the sound of his car. Sat in the boat, oars stowed, waiting, half sick of this lovelorn poaching. The wind came up and blew the boat west, parallel to the shore, and bless that dog if she wasn't waiting for me where my boat blew in. Eyebrows like karri moth wings in the dark, stepping into the water to greet me. Not a lover, not a life partner, not even a fisheries officer. Just a dog, watching out for me in the night, waiting for me to come ashore.

I walked through the bush today to Clarkie's rumoured hideaway. A rectangle of stone footings covered in bright green moss and sprinkled with tiny orange fungi is all that is left of Clarkie's Camp. It is about three metres by four and a slender peppermint tree meanders from the centre. I found no hearth but surely there was one, once. This small rectangle seems to be all that is left of his existence. I stood there, patted the tree and looked out to The Cut, where the sandbar guards against a huge, raging sea. Ninety years ago, a man was sentenced by law or fear of death to slide like a needle into the veins of this inlet. Maybe. It must have felt like being tipped off the edge of the world.

An owner from one of the shacks at Broke handed me a yellowed newspaper article from the 1970s. LIVING IN THE BUSH IN FEAR OF HIS LIFE, ran the headline. It told the story of Clarke, living out his days at Broke Inlet as a secret, a refugee consigned to the witness protection program for the rest of his life, and who'd eventually died in an insane asylum in Perth. I recognised the journalist's name and so I posted a photograph of the article on Twitter and added the handle of the journalist who'd gone out to Broke to write that story forty years ago. He was enjoying a quiet Sunday afternoon in Sydney when I rang him.

'Jesus, Sarah,' he said. 'I thought I'd lived that story down. It's the one story I got so wrong. And here you are today. *Posting it on Twitter!* We journos always want to get it right, yes? But straight after I published that story, three men came into the office, separately you know, they came in to say, "This Clarke you write of is not the same man. I knew Clarke and he was a different man from the Clarke involved in the coppers' murders." My dad, d'you remember his work? He was a journalist too. Had a column in *The West*. He put the two Clarkes together and I believed him. What else does a son do? Of course, I believed him. We were all wrong. It just wasn't true.'

We drink spiced rum. When the inlet temperature rises above twenty degrees there is fire in the water and so we row out to the rocks where we can see it dancing beneath us.

'Row,' the lover whispers to me. I row and watch our dogs swimming in the wake, their legs and bodies a shimmering fantasia of phosphorescence. He chugs from the bottle of rum and passes it to me. He pushes up my skirt and kisses my ankle, the inside of my knee. I stop rowing and the rum is hot in my throat. Tiny waves talk against the sides of the tinny.

We find the net's buoy in the dark. The dogs' paws shine in the sea, their tails a silvery wake. We pick up the net. Sea mullet flashing silver in my headlamp. The odd bull herring. Some whiting the size of my forearm. We row back to shore where the hurricane lantern hangs from a tree, and there we play in the shallows for a while, dancing on the luminescent shores, thrilled by this magic, by those cool flames firing away from our underwater feet, drunk with the light, the spiced rum, our dogs and our bucket of fish.

I hear the swell outside The Cut, roaring every night. I'm alone every night now. There is no resolution to the affair.

'It's my daughters,' he said to me through tears, when I realised he would never have the courage to tell the truth about me. The moral quandary over my part in my friend's death has not shifted. 'I have decided I shall die of shame,' my friend had said, rather grandly, considering his plans for the afternoon.

And I'll never be sure who Clarke actually was.

'Not the same Clarke,' said the journalist. 'Maybe a rumour started and Clarke of Broke Inlet enjoyed the notoriety. But he is not the same man.'

It strikes me that the term 'closure' is confined to certain personalities or situations. For the rest of us, closure is a beast that requires food, oxygen and movement. Anything less and it is stumbling towards the mortuary slab.

I woke at dawn a week ago knowing I shall leave the inlet soon. This country is magnificent. It is dynamic with natural drama, secret hideaways and tales operatic in their narrative and strangeness. The isolation has both served its purpose and done me in emotionally. I know that I need to wake in a place breathing with people again. No feral pigs, sketchy itinerants, rough shacks or monster dogs. Just a solid neighbour to lean over the fence and say, 'Morning, Sarah!'

Sexy old women – Krissy Kneen

On the 27th October, 2016, I finished a novel. It was a book I had been struggling with for a very long time. So many years in the making and finally I pressed the return key and wrote *the end* and watched the words standing strong and fierce out on their own, centred and following a double line break. I was near the end of a retreat with three other writers. We spent the days in comfortable silence, each of us bunkered down in our own temporary workspace. The house was near a wild beach, a strand full of broken branches, waves thundering down over rip-tides and deep gouges in the sandy bottom big enough to trip into. Our silent days were punctuated by walks on the beach, watching mother whales teach their daughters to leap and turn.

I watched the two words *the end* for a long while before quietly getting up from my desk, slipping a swimming costume on and walking down to the ocean. I didn't swim. It was impossible to do so. Instead I stood with the ocean pulling great swathes of sand out from under my feet, wondering if I had the courage to duck my head under the next ferocious wave. Of course I had the courage. I had just finished a very hard book. I could now do anything.

Back at the house I stepped out of my bathers and into the shower. It was only after my shower that I noticed the tiny rust-coloured drop in the crotch of my swimming costume. I had just got my period, timed perfectly with the finishing of a book. It was as if I had been holding on to the stress of everything whilst I finished the work. Those two words, *the end*, had released something inside me and I began to bleed.

What I didn't know at the time was that it would be my last menstrual cycle. It was the end of blood, the end of a long arduous stage of my life; the end of my book marked the end of my days as a fertile woman.

In my book *An Uncertain Grace*, we follow my main character, Liv, from her university days to her death at 130 years old and her consciousness beyond a life of the body. As you can imagine, it is a book set in the future, engaging with technologies that have not yet been invented. It is a book about sexuality and about the interdependence between sex and the body we live in. It was very important to me that my character Liv remained a sexual being right up until and beyond death. It was important to me because I am getting older. The older I get the more I see that the signifiers of sex are inextricably linked to youth. We say *young, sexy bodies*. We say *sexy young things*. We do not say *sexy old woman*.

Yesterday I stood next to my husband who was holding the tickets to a movie we were about to see. My husband is very fit, gently greying hair, well dressed, fine of feature. He is just six months younger than me. I am fat, unfit, scruffy, short, menopausal. The young girl took his tickets, saw that there were two of them, looked at him confused.

'Is your friend already in there?' she asked.

'No. This is my wife,' he said. She looked at me for the first time. I had been standing right next to him. She hadn't noticed me at all. Her eyes widened and she apologised. Embarrassed, she let us both go by.

What part of that list of descriptive words made me invisible to her? Fat, unfit, scruffy, short, menopausal? Maybe it was all of the above, but anecdotal evidence suggests that being old is enough to shield a woman from visibility.

In my day job I run book launches at Avid Reader Bookshop. I recently hosted an event with Helen Razer. She had written about dating as a middle-aged, recently single woman. She joked about how men of her age, mid-fifties, were joining online dating sites looking for women in their twenties and thirties. Newly single fifty-year-old heterosexual men rarely want to date fifty-year-old women.

In my book, Liv has sex with a young ungendered person when she is 129 years old. I read about telomeres in a *Scientific American*. Telomeres exist at the ends of chromosomes and as we age they wear down and become shorter. Gene therapy to extend and strengthen telomeres may mean extended and more active lives. One hundred years in the future, an active 129-year-old may not be such an odd sight. With this in mind, it was my job as a writer to describe the potential interaction. I needed to see Liv, to really see her in the act of sex, to make her body feel real for a reader, older than the oldest living woman in 2017 and also sexual. I looked to the great writers for help with this. Gabriel García Márquez wrote about an old man fantasising about a sexual encounter with a young virgin girl in *Memories of My Melancholy Whores*. Philip Roth hurled old man after old man onto the page, an annual literary parade of old men and their much younger female lovers. *Diary of a Mad Old Man* by Jun'ichirō Tanizaki, *The House of the Sleeping Beauties* by Yasunari Kawabata, Houellebecq, Carey, Nabokov. We have literary examples of sexual old men, but finding a model for a sexual older woman in literature proved to be a little harder.

Another anecdote: I was greeted at the front door of the Apple Store in Brisbane City by a young hipster guy with a big beard and facial piercings. He told me where to wait for a salesperson to help me pick the cable that I needed. I went to the wall of cables and waited. Other people were waiting. Sales people with hand-held tablets worked the area. They served the young girls in crop tops and high heels. They served the middle-aged man in a business suit. They served the young boy still in school uniform. They served the male hipsters and the nerdy female hipsters but they did not serve me. A girl raced past me with her tablet and I was forced to call out to her. 'Hey! I've been waiting over half an hour here.' She apologised but said she was busy. She would send someone to look after me. After another half an hour I left the shop empty-handed. I complained about it on my Facebook page and 125 women commented on my post. No, it wasn't just me. When you are a woman of a certain age you become invisible. Flirtation is half of sales work and who wants to flirt with a woman of our age?

I wake in the middle of the night. I am drenched in sweat. My heart is racing. What if I am pregnant? What if I don't have menopause? What if I left a tampon inside myself and that is why I haven't bled for three months? When I was in my twenties I once forgot my diaphragm inside my vulva. I felt like I had the flu. I had a fever, I felt terrible, and then I remembered that I had left the contraceptive device inside me. You need to leave it in for twenty-four hours after sex and I hadn't had a break in sexual activity all week and then I just forgot. It was a horrible experience and one that floods back to me now. I am hot, clammy, I don't feel right, my joints ache, my back aches, my lower abdomen feels crampy. I creep out of bed so as not to wake my husband and spend fifteen minutes feeling around inside me, wondering if there is a tampon in there somewhere just beyond my fingers.

No. Probably not. But I spend the rest of the night wondering about a late-life pregnancy, a geriatric pregnancy they call it. A geriatric pregnancy is a term used to describe pregnancy in women over thirty-five. I am nearing fifty. What would I do? It would be my last chance to have a baby. I have never wanted to have a baby. I don't want to be a parent, especially not now. These days when the sun comes up I am exhausted. I get up, bleary-eyed, fumbling around to find some clothes to wear to work. When I was thirty I used to be the first out of bed, sitting on the step with a hot coffee watching the sun rise, buzzing with the possibilities of a new day.

Mario Vargas Llosa wrote an erotic novel called *In Praise of the Stepmother*. In it Lucrecia is a happily married woman who begins a sexual relationship with her pre-teen stepson. This transgression almost brings down her happy marriage. In *The Graduate* by Charles Webb, which was made into a very popular film, a young man, Benjamin, has an affair with an older woman. The book ends with Mrs Robinson becoming jealous of Benjamin's relationship with her daughter. She becomes enraged and tries to destroy their lives. The cautionary message is unavoidable. In fairytales as in real life, the stepmothers, crones and older women are best avoided. They are dangerous, manipulating, clever enough to cause a man's downfall.

Sexual desire for the old is so unusual in our culture that sex researcher Krafft-Ebing invented a term for it in his book *Psychopathia Sexualis – gerontophilia*, which means a sexual attraction to the old. There is another term for young men who have a sexual attraction to older women, *anililagnia*. These are 'paraphilias', atypical sexual interests, anomalies, perversions of what is right and normal.

When I was young, I was at a queer film festival and they were screening the documentary *Nitrate Kisses* about the history of LGBQTI in the USA. In the film there is a scene where two very old lesbians engage in sex. There is a quite graphic fisting scene. I remember being shocked and surprised by the audience reaction as everyone squirmed and a loud synchronised 'ewwww' echoed through the theatre. It was such a strong and unified reaction from the audience. I couldn't understand why. Sure the women were wrinkled and old but their love was gentle, caring and quite frankly, beautiful. I was still young enough to think about my old age as something in the mythic distance but

I hoped that as an old woman I would be equally sexually bold. I walked out of the cinema and saw the audience in the light of day and was disturbed by how young we all were. Young and queer and equally closed-minded as all those heteros who marginalised us on a daily basis. I walked through the Queen Street Mall in the bright light of day and looked at all the older people. All the beautiful older people. I wondered about their secret sex lives. I hoped they were all still having wonderful, transgressive sex.

My character, M, who is transitioning away from gender, falls into sexual love with 129-year-old Liv. M is an outlier in their own way. Sex with ungendered M is a perversion of a different kind. When I began to write this scene I had to imagine my experiences with the older women in my life. I thought of my grandmother in the months before she died. I thought of the women in a nursing home I once did an arts project with. I thought of myself, of the changes that are already beginning to happen in my body, of my skin which is folding over on itself, drying out, becoming like parchment, of my back which hurts every day when I get out of bed and which continues to hurt even when I am lying down. Of the wakeful nights where I am enervated, sleepless, wondering how my childlessness will impact on my life when I am on my deathbed. Knowing that despite the frequent diets and worry about my weight, I will probably die fat, and knowing I have wasted years of emotional energy beating myself up about my appearance. I am also in a body outside the norm. I am moving further into this uncharted territory as I age, as is my character M who is transitioning to the centre between male and female. In this space outside the norm, M, the character, and I, the writer, watch Liv disrobe.

> She is standing in her bra and pants. It is a push-up bra, I notice, and she unsnaps it at the front and when she takes it off her breasts gentle down and flat against the bones of her chest. The nipples are pulled tight like two little pebbles, hard and dark on the paper thin skin...I know what I want now. I gently push her hands away and I hug her to me. Her nipples rub against mine as I walk her back against the bank. I carefully hold the cheeks of her arse in my hands. Jellyfish skin. It ripples against my fingers. I lift her and she is light as a piece of tissue billowing up with the movement of the water. I rest her down against me, shift my hips from side to side and her thighs float upward, exposing her to the press of me. I gently ease her down and my eyes close as her cunt closes around me. In her and out of her and in her again. Warm and cold. Alive and dead. Alive.

I check my reflection in the mirror. I never look at myself in the mirror anymore. I no longer take 'selfies', I don't share pictures of myself on Facebook. I try not to turn my head towards windows as I am walking by. If I refuse to look I can still pretend I am the person that I once was, thin enough to fit into regular dress sizes, young enough for shop assistants to flirt with. After writing the sex scene between Liv and M, I force myself to look. I disrobe.

I unclip the bra and let my breasts gentle down onto my stomach. It is hard to look at myself this way. Every day I walk past billboards and see magazines and watch television programs and read novels with characters that do not represent me. This is me. Here. Now. A fat, scruffy, menopausal woman. This is my body, all the dry folds of me, edged in skin that is beginning to wrinkle. I move my hands to my crotch and make small circles with my finger on my clitoris. I have been reading about menopause. My orgasms may diminish in intensity. My vagina will be dry. I resist the urge to close my eyes, to fantasise. In my fantasies I am always thinner, always younger. I keep my eyes steady and wide.

My breasts sway with my hand. I sit on the carpet and continue to watch the mirror. The swell of my flesh almost completely hides the tucks and folds between my legs. It is like a basket of bread rolls down there, swollen warm brown rounds of flesh. I find my mouth watering. I am not the same as I was. I will never be the sharp-edged, impetuous young girl again. But what I see has a different appeal: earthy, sensuous, slow. My body as a landscape has areas of interest, and it trembles as I rub it. It rises, it reddens, it swells. My body quakes like a fault line and then my eyes are shut or turned up to the sky but I don't see the moment of orgasm. I just feel it. I still feel it. Maybe it is gentler. Maybe it is quicker. It is hard to tell. I sit in the aftermath and know that I will be okay. Like Liv, the character I have just created, it is possible to be aroused by what my body is still capable of. I am older. But even in my social invisibility, even if the world refuses to know what I see, I am still a sexy old woman for all that.

On relationships – Brigid Lowry

Babies are a beacon of joy and delight. They also cry a lot. Perhaps it's because they sense what lies ahead: picnics, pets and library books, but also mean people, racism, climate change, old age, sickness and death. The full catastrophe, the entire crazy disaster.

After babyhood comes being a child. Some childhoods are happier than others. If you're lucky, you will survive your early life without extensive damage to body or spirit. It is a time of growing into yourself. You decide which foods you like, which books, which games. Next, the teenage years, which are, in the main, tricky. This time of angst and wonder is followed by attempting to be an adult. You marry, or not. You make babies, or not. You make friends, make bread, make mistakes, turn fifty, lose your way and find it again. You learn to play the cards you've been dealt.

One day you wake up and realise you are old.

Some days you feel young: zesty, happy, energetic. Sometimes you feel ancient: tired, in pain, world-weary. You attend funerals, staring mortality in the face, your own and other people's. You try to live the clichés: one day at a time, relax and enjoy, don't worry, be happy. Sometimes all you can manage is getting through the day with as much dignity as possible.

We are always in relationship: with our body, our feelings,

history, the earth, each other, the weather, our ancestors. There is no end to this list; there is nothing to which we are not in relation.

Thích Nhất Hanh, a Vietnamese Buddhist teacher, calls this 'interbeing'.[1] 'If you are a poet, you will see clearly that there is a cloud floating in this sheet of paper. Without a cloud, there will be no rain; without rain, the trees cannot grow; and without trees, we cannot make paper. The cloud is essential for the paper to exist. If the cloud is not here, the sheet of paper cannot be here either.'

Physics bears this out. All particles of matter are constantly shifting, each one affecting the others, in obvious ways and ways beyond our understanding. Relationships are not stable. They are a shifting energy flow, a puzzle that can never be solved. This is exciting, delicious and scary.

Sometimes it seems that the older we get, the less we are sure of. The mystery deepens. Certainties become less certain. We continue to wrestle with boundaries between self and other, with our need for approval, with our desires and aversions. What are we allowed to speak of, now that we are elders? Are sex, money and death suitable dinner conversation? Have we found a way of dressing which reflects us, neither dreary nor ridiculous? Are quinoa and spelt really superfoods, or are they just average grains with a high price tag and a clever marketing campaign? Do we really need the gym, pilates, physio, podiatry and aqua-aerobics? Maybe a daily walk, a dash of yoga and a dance around the living room will suffice? The ageing body continues to disappoint, as my friend Zoe says. No matter how hard we try, we can't avoid gravity or destiny, given the failing nature of the body. It seems unwise to take care of the body so religiously but forget to take care of the mind, flooding it with huge amounts of input that don't lead to tranquillity. For some, meditation is one more thing they can't find time for. For others, it's a force for good in a world going crazy. Peace and equanimity seem more valuable than expensive face products or a bigger TV screen. Each of us must choose to what degree we're willing or able to keep up with the fierce pace of technology. How much phone is too much phone? Is Twitter a bonus or just another time-thief making life more complicated? Some are early adapters, others are Luddites, while the rest of us muddle on with an increasing sense of bewilderment.

Going wider, we are all in relationship with the earth. The planet is struggling. Every aspect of our environment is at peril: species, climate, ocean, air. In what way do we contribute to this? Is it possible to rest easy at night while demanding cheap goods, bargain clothing and budget flights to far-flung destinations? Those of us in the first world have some serious decisions and sacrifices to make, because elsewhere the majority lack not only food and water, but basic human rights. As global citizens we can no longer ignore this relationship. We must change our connection to our lives and resources, in order to heal our ailing ecosystem for those who come next.

And then there's the simple matter of getting along with people, which is not always simple.

My own life is abundant with complex, marvellous relationships: with my granddaughter, with my son and his wife, my family of origin, former partners, friends, writing students, the motley crew who live in my retirement complex. Each of these connections offers joy, anxiety, comfort, solace, demands. They bring gifts I am not necessarily keen to receive: the suffering that ensues from tetchy exchanges, the angst of unreturned phone calls, times when someone else's troubles feel self-indulgent or the complexities of self and other seem too much to bear. I try to meet hard moments with equanimity, but sometimes I just take the phone off the hook and hide. I've learnt, from my Zen teacher, that to 'immediately do nothing' is often the best response. Sometimes all that's needed is to leave things alone.

There is no escape from the bump and grind of this life. We are born, we live, we die. All of us, headed for the boneyard. No-one exempt. This is the way things are. And in the midst of it, hell can be other people, as Jean-Paul Sartre pointed out. Or perhaps hell is ourselves. Our primary relationship is with our own hearts, bodies and minds, and this fertile, fluid inner territory abounds with contradictions. Many of us dance to a song we don't always recognise or enjoy. Sometimes it's difficult accepting oneself, let alone anyone else. When the shit hits the fan, can I behave towards other people in ways that reflect my beliefs? How do I deal with my shame and guilt when I stuff up? When shabbiness and shadow are revealed, the suffering can be immense.

As I have grown older, I understand more deeply that my relationship with the outer world waxes and wanes. Sometimes I feel deeply connected with other people, sometimes I don't. This calls on me to trust the emergence of what needs to unfold. It also requires me to examine, in a clear light, the limits of what I bring to relationships as well as the limits of what I can expect. I'm judgemental, controlling, prone to impatience. I can be a hopeless listener, too keen to interrupt, to fix, to solve, or to add my troubles to the mix. I'm also loyal, trustworthy, generous and, at best, a whole lot of fun. I value my friendships, despite the fact that many of my friends are getting a bit forgetful and don't always get back to me when I would like.

Surprisingly, I find myself with a new partner, a man of seventy. He's a kind, gentle, decent man whose life has not been easy, surprised and delighted to be taking one final ride on the merry-go-round of love. We talk, late at night, sharing stories of our marriages, our children and grandchildren, our victories and tragedies. He looks for the similarities between us, which are many. I am more conscious of our differences, also many. Taking on a new intimate relationship later in life is both wonderful and perilous. There's no biological or financial imperative involved, which removes certain pressures, but there are many challenges. Flexibility is important and brain plasticity has been proven, but how many new tricks are old dogs prepared to learn? With long roads of personal history behind us, it can be difficult to change one's views and habits, yet constant adaptation is necessary if one is to forge a harmonious relationship. Some days I bow down in gratitude to this man. Other days I could pick him up by the ears and shake him. No doubt he feels the same.

At our age, the stakes seem higher. Our aim is to be lovers at the deepest level, or why bother? With time so precious, meaningless flings and loveless marriages are no longer viable options. Together we explore the tender space between us, carving out a new territory, our own form of relationship, somewhere between married and single. It is vulnerable territory, at times almost unbearable. At best, it offers the freedom of room to move, along with companionship, comfort, physical pleasure and intellectual stimulation. At worst, we find ourselves lost in treacherous places of misunderstanding. Sometimes we are two gracious adults, relating with wisdom and ease. At other times, broken children, thrashing around in our own damage, not understanding the depths of our own wounding, blind to the frailties of the other.

In a primary relationship, ups and downs are more obvious, but pleasure and pain are manifest in all relationships. Sometimes we get on well with other people, sometimes we do not. In the end we're all just bozos on the bus, doing the best we can. As elders, we reconcile ourselves with our lives, nourishing the connections we have, whilst mourning relationships no longer available to us. It's an inescapable truth that grief is the price we pay for love. No matter how hard we try to rearrange the deckchairs on the *Titanic*, one day we will bury the ones we love, or they will bury us, except in the unlikely eventuality that we all go down together. The whole shebang has been on fire since the word go, as Annie Dillard reminds us, and it is no wonder that we feel screwed up a lot of the time and need to watch junk TV and eat yoghurt vacantly in front of the refrigerator, spilling the odd blob on the floor.[2]

In my thirties, I wrote the following:

> Sometimes I think I am so tired because I am
> a woman in a time and a place where no-one
> knows who they are any more, that I am utterly

worn out from thrashing around amongst so many discourses that all my strength is gone. For I am many, multiple, fractured. I am fat lady / thin lady / mother / lover / lone ranger / student / suburban housewife / consumer / ecologist / radical / conformist / hippie / yuppie / feminist / wife / shygirl / loudmouth / hedonist – and that is just a few of me, and I am tired.[3]

Thirty years later, still tired, I am all those things, and more. Grandmother, elder, Zen student, artist, sister, aunt, cook, friend, wise woman, fool. Human being in relationship with self and other: sky, tree, planet, child, ocean, teapot, moon and star.

So, what have I learnt along the way? As much as possible, to stop buying things. To live the simple life I proclaim, with a spirit of contentment, thus aligning my behaviours with my deepest values. To enjoy my life of divine ordinariness. To treat those I meet kindly, because we are all struggling, although some disguise it better than others. I have learnt that to be human is to be always in a state of flux, and that if I can live as change, as grace, my heart will be happier, despite global warming, shark attacks, terrorism and child poverty, despite my bung knee and my tendency towards melancholy. I aim to act for the wider good, while realising that my jurisdiction is limited. I try to be harmonious with my friends, even and especially when it proves difficult. I've realised it's not too late to have a happy childhood because, despite my own ragged past, I now get to play runaway horses and magic castles with my granddaughter. There's not much percentage in looking back, regretting old loves, nursing ancient hurts. Wiser to leave the past alone. Again and again, I farewell everything, including my ideas about myself. Staying current, inhabiting this moment, each moment, as the one and only real thing. Laying full claim to it, this precious, difficult, dizzying existence.

Notes

Thanks to Zoe Thurner for her great line.

[1] Thích Nhất Hanh, *Awakening of the Heart: Essential Buddhist Sutras and Commentaries*. Berkeley:Parallax Press, 2012.

[2] Annie Dillard, 'On Foot in Virginia's Roanoake Valley', *The Abundance*. London: Canongate Books, 2016.

[3] Brigid Lowry, 'Fat Lady', *Summer Shorts 2*. Fremantle: Fremantle Press, 1994.

What took me so long? – Pam Menzies

High heel shoes remain in their boxes, my hair is a puff of undyed white. I've never felt so free. Family, friends and being true to myself are what matter now. I no longer care what people think – I'm standing up and speaking out. My father would turn in his grave.

It's sunny but windy when we arrive in Sydney's Martin Place. We're here to prepare for a rally. Truckloads of men are jackhammering in the space we've booked and we haven't a clue what to do next. It's a new experience – I'm seventy and have never organised a protest. Three weeks before, I'd said to my friend Jan, a seasoned campaigner, I was cranky at the lack of political action on climate change. I told her it was the one thing I was prepared to take a stand on. A week later she phoned and said, 'If we are going to do anything we have to do it now before the July election; after that no-one will be listening. What do you say to the twenty-second of June?'

I grew up in the 50s, when girls spoke only when spoken to and we were warned 'not to have tickets on ourselves'. We knew our place, and never called our parents – or any other adult – by their first names. School was a mixed experience. At Port Kembla Primary, I ducked as Mrs

Cross let fly with inkwells, and didn't recover from Mrs Moe's criticism of my chain stitch sampler. She told me I would never sew because I was left-handed. (She was right about that, though neither she nor I could have foreseen that I would marry a man who did all my sewing.) The weekly tests that decided where you sat in class left me terrified of exams. I clung to one of the four back desks with two Sues and a Robyn: fourth on that slippery slope was as far as I was prepared to fall.

To gather support for our demonstration, we decide to target older people, as we think it's time our age group got active about climate. If we are willing to protest, politicians on both sides won't be able to opt out by saying it's a young person's issue. Jan fills in the rally permission form at her local police station and we're surprised how easy it is to get going. Neither of us has much idea about modern day protest strategies, so I ask young family members and their friends for advice. They tell us we need to design a slogan, set up an online petition on change.org, email our friends, start a Facebook page and above all have a photograph of ourselves taken. Apparently no-one will be interested unless there's a photo. We start with that as we find the rest challenging, though who knows why a photo of white-haired women is necessary.

Jan lives in Moss Vale in NSW; I live for most of the time in Sydney, but my husband and I own a small house on bushy acres nearby in the Southern Highlands, which we visit every few weeks and that's where we happen to be when the urge to get active hits. John, my hobby artist husband, finds an old canvas in the shed and whitewashes it. It's a bit rough, but will have to do. He paints on it the words THERE IS NO PLAN(ET) B, a popular slogan suggested by my daughter's friend Margo who works in advertising.

We call into Jan and Robert's on the way back to Sydney, find a colouring maple as a backdrop and Robert photographs us holding the sign. It's an au naturel affair with no attention to hair, make-up or clothes. We're running a 'what you see is what you get' campaign.

When I log on to change.org, I quail. This is going global; what if I mess it up? We've thought of a heading – 'Grandparents For Action On Climate' – and Robert has set up a gmail account for us. I follow instructions and am pleased when I manage to upload our maple tree picture and write a brief explanation about what we want from protesters and politicians. This online stuff is not too hard, I'm thinking, but realise I've only half done the job when an internet friend emails: 'Where's the accompanying letter to send to politicians with petition names?'

In sixth class, I escaped the strict confines of primary school for a secondary school in Wollongong, on acres of land with a creek running through. I was supremely happy in that idyll, yet nobody there encouraged me to aim high. Turning out ladies was the aim of the institution: our days were filled with elocution lessons, community service, gloves and hats, hockey and hurdles, and an eccentric collection of teachers. The history teacher's brother had been in the desert with Lawrence of Arabia and we spent hours obsessing about the romance of it all. In my final year the career advisor suggested teaching or physiotherapy. 'No thanks,' I told her. I had a father who believed sending girls to university was a waste of taxpayers' money because they would be married soon afterwards. I knew I needed to be charged up about something before he would change his mind, and I wasn't. Without other plans, I began working at the local hospital in the pathology department. I quite liked biology but my passion was literature.

There were reasons for my compliance. My choice of a non-vocational university degree would have displeased my father and I was very close to my mother as a child. We enjoyed the same things – animals, reading, music – and loved talking for hours. I believed it was up to me to make up for past sadness that occurred before I was born. In the first year of her marriage, her parents died and she had a stillborn son. A year later, a second son was born deaf. My mother was also preoccupied with being abandoned and often said, 'Everyone I've loved has gone away.' To go to university, I needed to live in the city and, at seventeen, I felt guilty about leaving her.

There's a fortnight to go before the protest. The next step is to persuade friends and acquaintances to join us in Martin Place. We send emails to everyone we know. The Knitting Nannas group from the Southern Highlands are coming, Ali, from Robert's choir, has agreed to lead us in the singing and a small core group of friends have agreed to be there. Other friends who support us, but for a variety of reasons can't come, send positive messages and help in different ways. In response to the email barrage, however, there's mostly silence.

Maybe I'm still seeking answers for the lack of support

from my age group when I venture into the Men's Shed near my gym a week before the protest. Four men are working. One is using a ruler to measure a piece of wood. There are chairs waiting for repair and there's a busy, convivial, under-control feel about the space.

'What have you got there?' one asks me.

'A flyer, we're holding a protest.'

'What about?'

'Grandparents, we want immediate action on climate.'

'I'm more interested in what's going to happen to my super,' one says.

'But you must care about the climate. Especially for your grandchildren.'

'How can I do anything about that?' says another.

'Tim Flannery has positive ideas in his new book and lists alternative energy sources.'

'Oh him, what would he know?'

'Oh well, I'd better let you get on with your work.'

'Give it to me,' one says, 'I'll put it up.'

Why did I go in there? Why were they unhelpful?

My husband suggests: 'When older men don't know the answer they stonewall to close down discussion.'

Two years after leaving school, I escaped my father's orbit and began working at Sutherland Hospital, where I met Sandra. She was my age, but light-years ahead when it came to decision-making. In charge of the biochemistry department, she drove an MG sports car and organised a loan to buy an apartment – unheard of in the 60s for a woman on her own. We flatted together – no tables or bedsteads, just mats and cushions. My father brought his own chair when he visited with my mother. Sandra taught me many things: to drive a car, to be more assertive and how to have fun as a young woman. She went on to study medicine.

For our protest Jan and I need to find a speaker with credentials. We're relieved when Michael Mobbs agrees. He is known as 'the off-the-grid guy' and has written books on sustainable housing. From media, on the whole, there's a big fat silence. I've written to ABC, Seven, Nine and ABC Radio – nothing, though Lauren Strode from Southern Highlands News is interested, and Elizabeth Farrelly, a journalist with Fairfax, writes a supportive email. A few days before the rally, I walk past Sydney's Supreme Court and see vans humming; they're from all the major television channels. Men are busy with cables, roof satellite dishes are swishing this way and that picking up signals and I almost dare to hand out my protest flyer, though know it would be pointless. I find out later they're covering the sentencing of a corrupt former cop.

My journey towards a stronger self-belief was helped by my husband John, whom I met at Sutherland Hospital. Two years and one child into our marriage, he said, 'You love reading, why don't you study for an external degree through New England University?' At the same time I met Barbara who was finishing a master's degree in education while producing many children. She was living a life I aspired to. And it turned out that reading, writing, talking about books and later, at Sydney University, studying performance, were a perfect fit for me. All through the 70s I soaked up words. Reading Anne Summers' *Damned*

Whores and God's Police made me bolshy for a while – the blinkers were off, and Germaine Greer completed the awakening. I began channelling my new knowledge. In Sydney, while my children were young, I worked part-time as an information officer at a community centre and came across local activism. There was a committee which organised after-school care for children and services for older people isolated in their homes, which was all new at the time. I also went to Women's Electoral Lobby meetings with my next-door neighbour Gillian, and joined the local P & C.

The day of the protest, Michael Mobbs suggests I ask the jackhammering workers if they will take their lunchbreak at twelve. They're quite happy about that and amble to the footpath to check out the commotion on Macquarie Street where taxi drivers are driving past, blowing their horns. They are agitating for better conditions for cabbies in support of the group gathered outside NSW State Parliament House across the road. We realise we're in the middle of protest central: groups of police are there, the taxi drive-past is slowing traffic and we decide to use the mood to begin. Before we do, two policemen come to check our credentials, little knowing they're making our day: we're bona fide now. With Bill McKibben's American campaign against the Keystone XL pipeline in mind, I'm hoping for drama, but these men are young and benign and say they wish all protesters were like us. There are fifty of us gathered and we shelter next to the Reserve Bank – in the sun and mostly out of the wind. We check out each other's posters. Anna's NO COAL MINING! created by her actor husband has a theatrical flair to it. We're impressed by Lyn's large banner that calls on us to be CUSTODIANS and PROTECT OUR LAND, WATER AND FUTURE.

Using the microphone, I welcome supporters repeating Elizabeth Farrelly's words: 'Survival is not a left-wing issue. The Queen, the Pope and John Hewson all warn of climate change catastrophe if not properly considered.'[1] Jan speaks brilliantly on what's facing us if we don't act. Then it's time for Ali to lead us in the singing of Bob Dylan's 'Blowin' in the Wind' with words altered by Jan for our purpose:

> How many seas must a seagull sail
> Before she sleeps in clean sand?
> How many plastic bags will be sold
> Before they're forever banned?

Michael Mobbs takes the mike and congratulates us for organising the event. He draws an analogy between past generations sending children to the First World War and sending current generations into the future of climate change catastrophe. We're on a roll; after another of Dylan's songs, 'The Times They are A-Changin'', Jan suggests we bus down to Canberra and sing to our federal politicians as a possible next move.

At thirty-nine, finally following my school counsellor's advice, I began teaching English at an all-boys school. I had a career as well as three cherished children. On her visits to our house, my mother-in-law tut-tutted, noting the absence of fresh flowers – I laughed, knowing the importance of work for me compared with home titivation. Learning professional skills helped develop a belief in myself in a way motherhood didn't. I was one of only four female teachers at the school when I started. It was tricky, negotiating my way through a predominantly male environment, and I was no strict disciplinarian. But I decided if I couldn't be myself, I'd have to give up. I'd learnt this the hard way at Marrickville High while doing my training for my Diploma of Education. I was in the middle of a history practical and my supervisor was sitting at the back of the classroom. I tried to rub notes off the whiteboard: no-go – the boys had replaced my marker with a permanent one. Trying to ignore this setback, I moved on to another topic. But the tall, bearded supervisor lost his cool and, taking one large leap, was in front of the class and telling them off: 'You don't know how lucky you are ...' Then he stormed out. The class and I were stunned: had I failed or had they? Later in the term, for my farewell, they closed the classroom blind, produced a supersize pink iced cake made by one of them and a card with a large red tiger drawn on it with the words 'Mrs Menzies, be a tiger to your students.'

During twenty years of teaching I found my way round bad behaviour without losing my sense of humour. Once I stood between two boys threatening to throw desks at each other, calmly asking them to put them down. They did, which was lucky – if they hadn't I might have lost my head.

Now retired, I'm ready for a different kind of action. Our demonstration is winding up and the police are hovering. One wants to know how long we'll be occupying the space, a notebook ready for my details: date of birth, phone number, etc. I ask if she'll wait, because as MC I need to listen and respond. 'Of course,' she says. 'I'll come back later.' Barristers spill out of the courts for their lunchbreak and a friend arrives, sorry to have missed the singing. Over the road, cabbies disperse; another day of protests is over. We pack up our placards, exhilarated we've found our voices. There's a huge climate change rally on Sunday, and we'll be there – activated now – never too old to stand up and speak out.

Notes

[1] www.smh.com.au/comment/natures-called-our-bluff-and-we-cant-keep-ignoring-it-20160609-gpfdwg.html

Everyday sadness – Liz Byrski

I was in my mid-fifties when I began to think seriously about ageing – about becoming an old woman and what that might mean. I did so with a kind of relish, for I had never feared growing old. Confident, intelligent and energetic old people were part of my childhood; I envied their independence and freedom and wanted to be like them. Childhood was all about doing what one was told; old people did what they wanted when they wanted, even if someone had already cautioned them against it. It was the late 1950s, I was just into my teens, and the older women I knew had just enough money to eat in restaurants, take the ferry for holidays in France or Spain, and go regularly to the best hairdresser in the nearest small town – some even drove their own cars. As an only child, inclined to introversion and protective of my own space as well as my dreams, old age shone like a beacon in the distant future.

But even as I grew older it simply never occurred to me to think about how it might actually *feel* to be an old woman; how emotionally textured, how sometimes ragged with grief and stitched through with loss or regret, how physically and mentally challenging, it could be. I was going to have a happy old age, and as the years passed I remained convinced of this.

When was it that the current inane cult of happiness began? Whose idea was it that we should expect to be happy all the time, and that to be sad was some sort of failure of will or personality? Sadness is so much more interesting, rich and lasting than this infernal happiness. Indeed, it is sadness or nostalgia rather than happiness that that moves us when we respond to the world's greatest works of literature, art and music – and sadness that has been their progenitor. We have come to despise sadness, to regard it as burdensome, negative, even as a sign of failure, and so we deprive ourselves of its value.

Now, in my seventies, I am living the good old age in which I so long believed, but in many ways it is not quite as I imagined it. Alongside all the benefits that I yearned for in youth, come the realities hidden for so long in my blind spot. In the course of an adult life we all experience grief, disappointment and loss. And I have kicked many own goals on the scoreboard of regret: broken relationships and friendships, roads not taken, opportunities missed, selfishness, cowardice, greed and neglect. But it was the reality of my parents' ageing that helped me to understand the importance and the value of both grief and regret.

My father was in his early eighties, becoming very forgetful and sometimes confused, when a minor stroke catapulted him further along the road to dementia and a diagnosis of Alzheimer's disease. My mother, who had always depended on him for everything, was confused and frightened by this, and resentful that he was no longer able to look after her. The familial triangle rocked in chaos. The old structure, at times suffocating and restrictive, at others liberating and supportive, shifted on what felt like a daily basis, as we grasped for the past and found it slipping from our hands.

I became my parents' carer shortly after my sons had left home. I had a demanding job, a busy social life, and was free of other responsibilities, so I bitterly resented this new one. My parents had always tried to do their best for me, so resenting having to take responsibility for them is not something I'm proud of; it reveals a dark and selfish aspect of my nature which I'd prefer to hide. But I know I'm not alone in this experience and perhaps if we can speak more freely about our reactions, which feel so shameful, it might be easier to manage them. Alongside the resentment, I struggled with the long slow grief of watching Mum and Dad become people I barely knew. And as they disappeared before my eyes I hated myself for my selfishness. I always knew that my parents loved me, but in my twenties I had begun to understand that they only tolerated each other. Our apparently perfect middle-class family life, serene on the surface, was laced with unspoken resentment and tension. Like so many only children I believed that it was up to me to fix this, that if I was exceptionally good and did well at school, the centre would hold, things would not fall apart.

Things didn't fall apart, but reflecting on it now I realise I never really knew or understood either of my parents. So much went unspoken, so much was hidden, that in the final years of both their lives I felt that not only had I never really got to know them, but as an adult I had not allowed them to know me. At some point in my adult life, probably in my thirties, I stopped talking to them. It wasn't that we weren't speaking, just that I started editing the version of myself that they saw. We had profound political differences by then, and there were aspects of my life that I knew they would disapprove of, or might hurt them. And so I turned the flame of intimacy down to a flicker, stopped disclosing my plans, my failures, my hopes or aspirations. I didn't tell them of the times I fell in love and rapidly out of it again, or when I walked the boundaries of financial disaster. I didn't confide concerns about my children in case that reflected badly on me. Somehow I still felt I could only hold the triangle together by living up to their expectations and, although I saw them often and loved them deeply, I never revealed my failures, shortcomings, weaknesses or fears. From being at the centre of their lives I moved myself out to the emotional margins.

My regrets about my parents are many, and foremost among them is my failure to heed the advice of others about the futility of trying to make a person with dementia understand and accept what is 'real' and 'correct'. I argued too long, too forcefully and too often with my father. When he told me something outrageous or simply incorrect I insisted on putting him right. It was a useless and frustrating exercise and, worse still, once he was gone I realised that it undermined him at a time when he was most vulnerable. In earlier days I had frequently resented his authority and, even as an adult, I rarely summoned the courage to argue with him. But when he was old and sick I argued with him constantly. Now I wonder if this was some sort of unconscious revenge in which I sought the triumph of being the one who, supposedly, knew best. Once he was gone, I saw how easy it would have been to change the dynamics of that relationship earlier, at a time when we could have enjoyed each other's differences. How much kinder it would have been to let him live with his harmless delusions, instead of trying to control his sense of himself and his reality. Regrets ... I have more than a few.

Regret is not fashionable; it is often regarded as useless or self-indulgent, but in recent years I've come to understand its value. I have learnt so much from both grief and regret – learnt my strengths and my weaknesses, my faults and mean-spiritedness, the things that cause me shame, and my readiness to compromise my beliefs and values when confronted by the difficulties they can create for me. To cast regret aside is to cast aside the chance to learn and change, and to try to live more authentically.

I still grieve for my parents, for the dear friends I've lost, and for the things I can no longer do: dance the night away, move freely without pain, stand in high heels, pull things out of my memory with ease, juggle several trains of thought at the same time, remember where I put my glasses, expect to fall in love. But other blessings come in their place, the greatest of which is what I have come to call 'everyday sadness', and what I can learn from it. I relish my solitude, my independence and the company of dear friends. And while I still care about how I look, I am no longer haunted by my failure to measure up to the sort of standards my mother would have approved of. I have learnt to live with my weight, my endlessly disappointing hair and my own fashion disasters. Varying degrees of pain, discomfort and days of exhaustion are just part of life. I am learning to accommodate rather than fight them.

To be old – to be present in one's oldness – is both the

great challenge and the great gift of time. Grief, regret and sadness are part of this. What seems at first to rob and weaken us moves us towards a stronger and more nuanced sense of self; one which enables us to inhabit old age rather than fight it; to embrace it rather than to grasp at youth. I am not a sad person; I am not unhappy, gloomy or depressed. But everyday sadness is simply a part of me now and I feel it as a gift, something that keeps me company, and guides me in the direction that may perhaps lead me along the road to some wisdom.

Recently I've been experimenting with everyday sadness, trying it out on people to see how they respond to it. People of my own age, and older, frequently understand what I mean. But many younger people seem shocked or horrified. 'But you should be happy!' they respond. 'You're not old; well, you don't look it.' 'It's terrible to be sad – and you can't be sad every day!' Well, actually I can, because this sadness does not make me miserable, it makes me strong, and it has become a precious part of being old. My everyday sadness lives within; hopefully it makes me more tolerant, more focused and compassionate. It alerts me to dishonesty and sophistry. It is a long time now since I recognised the damaging impact of the cult of happiness. The way it sets us up for disappointment, and the shame that comes with the failure to appear happy about everything all or most of the time.

I am feeling my age, I am learning what it means to be an old woman and I still have a considerable way to go. I wish people would stop telling me that I'm not old. I know they mean it kindly, and I know that sometimes it comes from their fear of their own ageing. But I am seventy-three and I'm proud of it. I don't want to be young again, I don't need to be told that I look younger than my age. I want to explore, discover and celebrate this time of my life, to live my age in my own bloody-minded way, to reflect and learn. I need this sadness to keep me strong and to enrich my appreciation of the everyday joy of living. I wonder now if this was what I saw in those old people of my childhood – what made me want what they had. I relish this time and reject the cult of happiness. I love being an old woman and I wonder if they had also found what I have found: that a little everyday sadness suits me very well.

Notes

A section of this essay has previously been published in *Getting On* (Momentum Books, 2012).

Contributors

Anne Aly was born in Egypt and immigrated to Australia at the age of two. She is an Australian politician, political scholar, academic and counterterrorism expert. She was appointed associate professor at Curtin in 2014, and then professor at Edith Cowan in 2015, and has been the Federal Member for Cowan since July 2016. Anne is the author of *Terrorism and Global Security: Historical and Contemporary Perspectives* and has written extensively about terrorism, counterterrorism and radicalisation. The essay in this collection is an extract from Anne's forthcoming memoir to be published by ABC Books in 2018.

Tracey Arnich is the eldest of four children. She is fifty-two years old, and the single mother of two children. She grew up in Tasmania but now resides in Perth, Western Australia. Her past careers have been included running nightclubs, valuing and cataloguing militaria, antiques, veteran vintage and classic motorcycles. Her present careers are fortune-telling and floristry. Tracey's hobbies are art, music, cooking and reading. She loves spending time with her family and friends.

Liz Byrski is the author of a number of non-fiction books including *Remember Me, Getting On: Some Thoughts on Women and Ageing*, and *In Love and War: Nursing Heroes*, as well as nine novels including *The Woman Next Door* and *Family Secrets*. She has worked as a freelance journalist, a broadcaster with ABC radio and as an advisor to a minister in the Western Australian Government. Liz is an Associate Professor in the School of Media, Culture and Creative Arts at Curtin University.

Sarah Drummond writes novels, short fiction, memoir and essays, and has been shortlisted for various Australian literary awards. She holds a PhD in history, and her work is imbued with character and a sense of place. She is the author of a non-fiction book, *Salt Story: Of Sea-Dogs and Fisherwomen* and a novel, *The Sound* (Fremantle Press, 2013 and 2016).

Dr Mehreen Faruqi joined the NSW Legislative Council in June 2013 and is the first Muslim woman elected to any parliament in Australia. Prior to this she was the director of the Institute of Environmental Studies at the University of NSW and an associate professor in business and sustainability. She is a civil and environmental engineer with twenty-five years experience working in local government, multinational consulting firms and academia. Since migrating from Pakistan to Australia in 1992 with her young family, she has worked across NSW with a focus on gender equality, inclusiveness and social justice. She is passionate about amplifying community voices on climate change action, environmental protection, and closing the gap on inequality.

Goldie Goldbloom lives in Chicago with her eight children. Her short fiction has appeared in many journals, including *Ploughshares*, *The Kenyon Review*, *Meanjin* and *Prairie Schooner*, and has been translated into more than ten languages. Her first novel, *The Paperbark Shoe*, won the US Association of Writers and Writing Programs' Novel Award, as well as being named Foreword Indies Book of the Year for Literary Fiction (published in the US as *Toads' Museum of Freaks and Wonders*). Goldie is the author of a collection of short stories, *You Lose These*, and a second novel, *Gwen*. She teaches at Northwestern University and the University of Chicago.

Krissy Kneen is the award-winning author of the memoir *Affection*, the novels *Steeplechase*, *Triptych*, *The Adventures of Holly White and the Incredible Sex Machine*, *An Uncertain Grace*, and the Thomas Shapcott Award-winning poetry collection

Eating My Grandmother. She recently won the *Griffith Review* Novella Project prize and an Australia Council fellowship. She has written and directed documentaries for SBS and ABC television.

Jeanine Leane is a Wiradjuri writer. She lectures at the University of Melbourne on creative writing and Aboriginal literature. Her novel, *Purple Threads*, won the David Unaipon Award in the 2010 Queensland Premier's Literary Awards, and was published by UQP. It was subsequently shortlisted for the 2012 Commonwealth Book Prize. Her book of poetry, *Dark Secrets*, won the 2010 Scanlon Prize for Indigenous Poetry. In 2017, she won two national poetry prizes: the Oodgeroo Noonucal Prize (co-winner) and the University of Canberra Aboriginal and Torres Strait Islander Poetry Prize. Her second poetry collection *Walk Back Over* was published in 2017 and she has just competed her second novel. Jeanine has also published widely in the area of Aboriginal literature and cultural appropriation.

Brigid Lowry has a master of arts in creative writing, and has published both poetry and short fiction for adults, as well as eight books for teenagers. *Guitar Highway Rose* and *Juicy Writing: Inspiration and Techniques for Young Writers* are two of her prize-winning YA titles. Her latest book is *Still Life With Teapot: On Zen, Writing and Creativity* (Fremantle Press, 2016). Brigid is a Zen student who believes in op shops, coloured pencils, vegetables, oceans, cake, floral frocks, postcards, and fostering joy and creativity in herself and others.

Pam Menzies is a passionate activist who organised her first protest at the age of seventy. As a younger person, she did everything to escape country life on the South Coast of NSW. Now older, she spends as much time as possible on a bushy block of land in the Southern Tablelands. An earlier version of this piece was published in *Overland* in 2016.

Jodie Moffat commenced her law degree the year she turned forty and graduated as a Juris Doctor at the age of forty-four. Her paper, 'Arranging Deckchairs on the Titanic', won the Morella Calder Memorial Prize in 2010, and was published in the *Australian & New Zealand Maritime Law Journal* that year. Jodie spent five years as a commercial litigator in the Perth CBD before taking up practice as a generalist solicitor with a community legal service in 2017. She ran as the Greens Party lower house candidate in her hometown of Mandurah in the 2017 state election.

Charlotte Roseby is a writer, editor and documentary film-maker. She works as a copywriter, getting in deep with a range of technical subjects. Charlotte's first film *Still Breathing*, seen on SBS TV, documents her friend Rob's moment of truth as he faces the decision to have a lung transplant. Her second film, *In the End*, featured on ABC TV's *Compass* program. It explores the consequences of modern medical advances in intensive care that are prolonging elderly patients' lives, when they are already well along the path of dying.

Maria Scoda is an experienced clinical and consultant psychologist who works in private practice in the Sydney CBD. She earned her doctorate in clinical psychology from the Australian National University in 2002. She also holds a bachelor of arts, with honours in psychology. In addition to her clinical work, Maria assists business executives to understand and manage complex relationship dynamics for better interpersonal relationships in the workplace and at home. She is regularly contacted by the media for professional commentary and opinion on psychological issues, such as relationships, anxiety and depression.

Jenny Smithson is a Commissioner of the NSW Land and Environment Court and a qualified town planner, being a Life Fellow and former state president and national councillor of the Planning Institute of Australia. She is a former senior principal of international consulting firm Cardno. She is a graduate of the Australian Institute of Company Directors and a former director of BSD Consultants, Cardno (WA), and LandCorp. Jenny was appointed by the WA Government as a commissioner to the Shire of Albany and to the City of Cockburn Councils. In 1996 she was a finalist for the WA Citizen of the Year for her contribution to the planning profession.

Susan Laura Sullivan writes fiction, essays and poetry. Her work has been published in *Westerly: New Creative, Plumwood Journal*, and *The Font: A Literary Journal for Language Teachers*, among others. She holds a master of creative arts, and has taught creative writing at Curtin University and to the general community. She was shortlisted for the T.A.G. Hungerford Award in 2012, and currently lives in Japan, where she teaches English.

Pat Mamanyjun Torres is an Australian First Peoples woman. Her ancestors are traditional owners of Djugun, Yawuru, Garajarri, Nyul-Nyul, Jabirr-Jabirr and Bardi lands in the areas around Broome, WA. Pat is passionate about the development of the Australian wild/native foods industry and its holistic engagement with Indigenous people, and she is committed to the 'good, clean and fair' Slow Food ethos for native foods in her region. She is a published author and illustrator, whose work has appeared in *Kimberley Stories* (Fremantle Press, 2012).

Acknowledgements

Women of a Certain Age was made possible due to the honesty and generosity of certain women of a certain age. The editors would like to thank our contributors for so willingly and completely sharing their stories with us.

Thanks to Georgia Richter, Naama Grey-Smith and the team at Fremantle Press whose enthusiasm and editorial expertise guided us through all stages of the book.

Jodie would like to personally thank Jeff, Earl, Argus and Uther, Tracy, Jenny, Michelle and Deborah, Patricia and Ronald, and all her nieces, nephews, cousins and friends who have supported and sustained her through the years, and in this project.

Maria would like to say a warm thank you to Andy Nehl, Val Scoda, Rob Scoda and Diana Bartolillo for their helpful feedback and useful conversations, and to Georgia Richter for her excellent advice.

Sue is indebted to her mother, Margaret Sullivan, and great-aunt, Margaret (Mag) O'Rourke, whose life experiences influenced the telling of her own story. She is grateful to her friends and family for their encouragement and input, and to the many others who contributed to the making of the book.

The three of us appreciate the inspiration and support we drew from one another that saw us through the editorial process. We'd like to thank the wisdom that comes with age, late-night Skype calls, and recognising that nearly everything goes better with a glass of wine, or if truly dire, a comparable quantity of chocolate.

More great reads

'brilliant and strange, compassionate and wild'
Audrey Niffenegger, author of *The Time Traveler's Wife*

Gwen

A NOVEL

GOLDIE GOLDBLOOM

available from fremantlepress.com.au

from Fremantle Press

A NOVEL BY
SARAH DRUMMOND

The
SOUND

You can feel the sea, the salt, the wind and jostling waves on every page of this impressive novel.
Kim Scott

as ebooks and at all good bookstores

STILL LIFE
with teapot
on zen, writing & creativity
BRIGID LOWRY

from Fremantle Press

This is a book about the heroes and heroines who unflinchingly met the demands and challenges of their day.

Professor Fiona Wood, AM

In Love and War
nursing heroes
Liz Byrski

as ebooks and at all good bookstores

First published 2018 by
FREMANTLE PRESS
25 Quarry Street, Fremantle WA 6160
(PO Box 158, North Fremantle WA 6159)
www.fremantlepress.com.au

Cover image: Alamy.com, EB3ENG
Printed by McPherson's, Australia

A catalogue record for this
book is available from the
National Library of Australia

Women of a Certain Age: Life stories from Anne Aly, Liz Byrski, Sarah
Drummond, Mehreen Faruqi, Goldie Goldbloom, Krissy Kneen, Jeanine
Leane, Brigid Lowry, Pat Mamanyjun Torres and others

ISBN: 9781925591149 (paperback)

Department of
Local Government, Sport
and Cultural Industries

Fremantle Press is supported by the State Government through the
Department of Local Government, Sport and Cultural Industries.

Publication of this title was assisted by the Commonwealth Government
through the Australia Council, its arts funding and advisory body.